CW00591492

Colin Elliott

LONG DISTANCE TRAILS ALMANAC

A WALKER'S REFERENCE BOOK

LOCHAR PUBLISHING • MOFFAT • SCOTLAND

© 1992 Colin Elliott

Published 1992 by
Lochar Publishing
The High Street
Moffat DG10 9ED
Scotland

British Library Cataloguing in Publications Data available upon request.

ISBN 0-948403-69-1

Typeset by Origination, Luton in 9pt on 10pt Times, and printed by Cambus Litho Ltd., East Kilbride

CONTENTS

To Jane, Tim and Kate,
best of walking companions
since birth, this book is
fondly inscribed by The Guv.

Acknowledgements

Thanks are due to the officials of various
organisations, particularly in many county and
district councils, who took trouble to answer
inquiries about long distance walking routes in
their areas. Their interest and enthusiasm revealed
a new and friendly face of local government.

Several friends and organisations helped with
photographs and these have been acknowledged
where they appear. Those not otherwise ascribed
are the author's own. My wife efficiently navigated
on research expeditions and checked the copy.

All the maps are by Peter Stuckey.

INTRODUCTION

The first thing that needs saying about long distance trails is that they are not intended to be endurance tests. If you fancy racing over one in a Royal Marine style 'yomp' the choice is yours, but the trails are there to be enjoyed in a variety of ways by people of all ages and inclinations and at any pace.

This book is a guide to the lifetime of pleasure that can be gained from them, giving essential details of the best in Britain's rich and varied landscape. For the experienced long distance walker this will aid the choice and planning of future expeditions and suggest interesting new country to explore. For others it will reveal a wealth of possibilities for holidays, week-ends and shorter excursions that they might not have realised existed.

Long distance trails are the most wonderful new recreational development this century. They have added a new dimension to enjoyment of the countryside and through them thousands of people are rediscovering the simple joys and benefits of walking, rambling, hiking, backpacking, call it what you will.

WHAT ARE LONG DISTANCE TRAILS?

We can go back to the Middle Ages to find evidence of the first people who undertook a long distance trek for enjoyment. These were the pilgrims who undoubtedly saw their journey to some distant holy shrine as a holiday as much as a spiritual exercise.

In modern terms the idea of a long distance trail probably originated with the 2,000 mile long Appalachian Trail in America, founded in 1921. The first one suggested in Britain was the Pennine Way, an idea of the writer Tom Stephenson in 1935, but it did not become a reality for over 30 years. Eventually it was designated the first national trail and a model for others. When the Countryside Commission and the Countryside Commission for Scotland were set up in 1968 they were charged with the responsibility of creating long distance footpaths and bridleways as part of their wider duty to protect the natural beauty of the country and make it more accessible for public enjoyment.

There is nothing artificial about these trails. They are created by planning routes along existing public footpaths and linking them up where necessary by negotiating new rights of way or permissive access with landowners, the route then being signposted and waymarked as necessary. Only in rare instances is a path laid out where none existed before. Even less are they artificially surfaced, except here and there to prevent erosion. A long distance trail simply makes it easier to walk in and explore the natural landscape, with a little sense of adventure that comes from not being reliant all the time on the internal combustion engine and other amenities of urban living. Somebody coined for them the phrase 'footpath touring' which is perhaps as good a description as any.

Three types of long distance footpath are included in this almanac:-

National trails.   Those created by the two Countryside Commissions who meet the whole cost of setting them up, waymarking, maintaining them and publishing relevant literature. Currently there are 14 in England and Wales and 3 in Scotland. Others are in the pipeline but will mainly come from taking over responsibility for existing trails in the other categories. You can expect to find these well marked (by an acorn symbol in England, a thistle in Scotland) and maintained, with plenty of information and printed guides books available.

Regional routes. Trails created by local authorities, usually the county councils, with the encouragement of the Countryside Commission who meet 50% of the cost. Some have taken an evident pride in developing distinctive local routes and there has been inter-county co-operation in taking trails across neighbouring boundaries. Usually local ramblers' groups have been closely involved in suggesting and pioneering the routes. Regional routes, of which there are now over a hundred, are generally well waymarked and kept, but standards in available information and printed guides vary from excellent to poor.

Unofficial trails. Long distance footpath routes devised by groups of walkers, such as local branches of the Ramblers' Association, or just by enterprising individuals. In most cases these simply make use of existing rights of way and there is no special waymarking, only normal 'Public Footpath' signs which might be absent in places. Neither will there be any special maintenance of tracks, stiles, gates, etc. Nearly always however there is a printed route guide available and several of the most popular long distance trails are unofficial. Some local councils have been persuaded to help these enterprises so that the 'unofficial' sometimes comes close to being 'regional'. About 200 are in existence.

USING THIS ALMANAC

The number of long distance paths has quite exploded recently and continues to grow, especially regional and unofficial ones (new national trails are a little slow in coming) so that any account of them all would be tedious to read and quickly out of date. This selection includes nearly all the longer ones and more popular ones, but the choice has also taken into account variety of landscape and representation of different areas of Britain. As a result the selection also includes many shorter and less well known trails.

Each entry gives the following information:-

Name & Length: Complete with sketch map showing line of route and general location.

Status: Whether national, regional or unofficial.

To & From: Beginning and starting points. These are usually interchangeable, but if there are particular reasons for prefering one end as the start this is stated in the description. If you choose the direction opposite to the one used by the author of the printed guide it can be tricky reading the directions 'backwards', but by no means impossible with the aid of an Ordnance Survey map.

Terrain: Briefly summarises the kind of countryside to judge how hard the wallking might be.

Maps: Sheet No's of Ordnance Survey maps in the 1:50000 Landranger series ($1^1/_4$ inches to one mile) needed to cover the whole route. When detailed printed guides are available these may not be essential, unless you are breaking up or varying the walk, but it is always advisable to have both map and compass in remote areas. Whether essential or not maps always add enormously to the pleasure of planning the walk, doing it, and enjoying it again in retrospect. Some enthusiasts may want the OS 1:25000 Pathfinder series (2^1/$_2$ inches to one mile), but space does not permit all these to be listed. Most bookshops stock OS maps for at least their own region and will order others at request.

Access: Gives the nearest railway station to the start followed by the best road approach for those going by car. The second line gives the same details for the finish. Most route guides give some public transport details for intermediate points for those doing the walk in stages, usually in the form of telephone inquiry numbers for railway stations and bus companies.

Route Guides: Gives titles, authors and publishers of those in print at the time of writing. Most can be ordered from any bookshop. If not try the address given under 'Information' in the line below. This mostly applies to those shown as published by councils.

Information: Best address for general information about the trail, including accommodation, camp sites, local transport, places of interest etc.

Description: A potted itinerary pointing out main points of interest en route and giving a general idea of the character of the trail.

WAYS OF EXPLORING A TRAIL

As indicated at the beginning there are more ways than one of enjoying trail walking. Each needs a different sort of planning so it is worth considering them.

End to End   This was undoubtedly the original concept and can induce a great glow of achievement. The examples in this almanac are suitable for anything from a week-end break to a long holiday. The longest, the South West Peninsula Coast Path, needs free time of five or six weeks to finish in one go. The majority of other longer ones will fit happily into a week, ten day or fortnight holiday.

Accommodation is the biggest consideration. Backpacking, in other words carrying a lightweight tent and sleeping bag is one solution. Bed and breakfast in villages and farmhouses is another. Arriving somewhere on spec. is fun and doesn't tie you down to a timetable, but it can be chancy and a bit tiring looking for somewhere at the end of the day, so there is a lot to be said for booking in advance. The Ramblers' Association Year Book contains a good acommodation guide. Addresses can also be obtained from the information sources given in each section and from all tourist offices. There are youth hostels in the vicinity of most trails and despite the name have no upper age limit. Membership of the Youth Hostels Association for a very modest subscription is all that is necessary.

An alternative on longer national trails is to go with a walking tour organisation which provides a guide, books overnight stays and transports your luggage from one point to another, which saves having to carry a heavy rucsac. These advertise in the back of magazines like *Great Outdoors, Country Walking* and *Rambling To-day*.

In Short Stages   Most trails can be divided into a number of shorter excursions and there is a lot to be said for spreading out the pleasure, for instance by doing a hundred mile route over a series of three or four week-ends. This is often a more convenient approach for people who do not want to devote a whole holiday to it because they have family and other commitments. The only problem this poses is one of transport to and from the intermediate stages, but with a little investigation this can usually be worked out, though a cautionary note has to be sounded about the infrequency of rural bus services in many parts. Of course spouses, relations or friends will often provide a chauffeur service and fit it in with some outing of their own. Arrangements with other walkers to take two cars, leave one at the end of a section and drive back in one car to the start, reversing the procedure at the end, can also work out well.

Making It Last For Ever   This heading is not as silly as it looks. A trail doesn't have to be finished and ticked off as complete. Some people find that one trail, perhaps not too far from home, can in itself become an absorbing hobby. They spend years walking it in day excursions, regarding it as a kind of linear country to explore. This way it is easy to become absorbed in its wild life, history, villages, architecture, churches and so forth. It doesn't even have to be walked in logical order.

Transport doesn't have to be a problem even if there are no non-walking friends able to provide a pick-up. This kind of trail walking lends itself to circular rambles, leaving the route and finding another way by public footpaths and country lanes back to the day's starting point. The latest generation of trail route guides make a point of including directions for these circular ambulations. Retracing footsteps in the absence of a viable circular route is not to be spurned as scenery often looks quite different the other way.

Record Breaking   Finishing in the fastest possible time is a pursuit in its own right and is known as challenge walking. Some organisations issue certificates and badges to people who like that sort of incentive. Done by small groups of individuals this is a harmless, healthy pastime, but unfortunately it produces a tendency to congregate large numbers of people on organised events which is environmentally damaging, especially on popular routes, as well as being antagonising to local communities.

ANGLES WAY

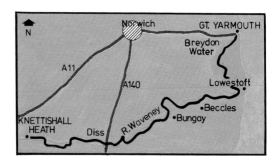

Length:	77 miles 123 kms
Status:	Regional route
From:	Knettishall Heath
To:	Great Yarmouth
Terrain:	Level river paths and fen
Maps:	OS Landranger 134, 144, 156
Access:	BR Harling Road via Norwich. A11 London-Norwich road BR Great Yarmouth. A45 from Norwich
Route guides:	*Angles Way* (Ramblers' Association)
Information:	Planning Dept, Norfolk County Council, County Hall, Martineau Lane, Norwich NR1 2DH

As flat and restful a long distance trail as you are likely to find and one of four which link in a continuous chain to make up a grand tour of eastern England. This one starts where the Peddars Way (q.v.) leaves off, in the Knettishall Heath Country Park, near Thetford, on the edge of a little explored region of Norfolk called the Brecklands. It follows the course of the Little Ouse and Waveney rivers, passing restored and working windmills at Thelnetham, Billingford and Herringfleet and a steam museum at Bressingham. The area is rich in wading birds and river life, including otters, and the route passes through three nature reserves preserving now scarce fenland habitat which is home to threatened species. Crossing over the border into Suffolk for a while it visits Bungay, with a ruined castle and fine Georgian architecture, and Beccles in whose grand church Nelson's parents were married. By now the route is really into the Broads country with plenty of activity on the water most of the year round. Oulton is the first large broad, just on the outskirts of Lowestoft whose ancient 'scores' (streets running down the harbour) are worth seeing. A diversion into the town will be necessary if you want to stand on the most easterly point of Britain, though unlike exploited Land's End it is tucked away unadvertised behind an industrial estate. The path heads north now to meet Breydon Water, really a bottled up estuary which is a Site of Special Scientific Interest. Beyond it is Great Yarmouth, both a seaside resort and busy port where the main Broads rivers run into the sea.

River Waveney at Beccles   *(Photo: Jarrold Publishing)*

AROUND NORFOLK WALK

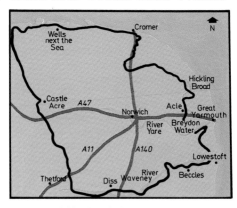

Length:	220 miles 352 kms
Status:	Regional & National
From:	Great Yarmouth (or other points)
To:	Return to start (circular)
Terrain:	Predominantly flat farmlands, coast, riverside and fen
Maps:	OS Landranger 132, 133, 134, 144, 156
Access:	BR Great Yarmouth. A45 from Norwich Other points can be reached by road or rail via Norwich
Route Guides:	See individual entries of trails mentioned below
Information:	Department of Planning, County Hall, Martineau Lane, Norwich NR1 2DH

This long trail round Norfolk is made up by the linking of two national trails (Peddars Way and North Norfolk Coast Path) and two regional routes (Angles Way and Weavers' Way). All are described in more detail in individual entries (q.v.). The Around Norfolk Walk can be started and finished, or broken off and resumed, at a number of easily accessible places. Great

Yarmouth is suggested here only for the sake of starting somewhere. To take the trail from there in a clockwise direction means first following the Angles Way along the south side of Breydon Water, past Oulton Broad and up the broad valley of the River Waveney, passing through handsome villages like Beccles, Bungay and Diss. Then it abandons the Waveney for the Little Ouse which it follows into the heathland area of Norfolk called the Brecklands. Here at Knettishall Heath, near Thetford, it meets the Peddars Way, the national trail based on an ancient roadway believed to have been built by the Romans to keep order after the uprising led by Queen Boadicea. To-day it is made up of green lanes and farm tracks across unpopulated country, passing through only one village of any size. Reaching the north coast brings a dramatic change of scenery - wild saltmarshes, tidal creeks, and sandy beaches which continue to the cliffs of Sheringham and Cromer. The last section is the Weavers' Way which goes through typical Broadlands villages, via Hickling Broad, Potter Heigham and Acle to the northern shores of Breydon and back to the start.

North Norfolk Coast   *(Photo: Ian Howard)*

CENTENARY WAY

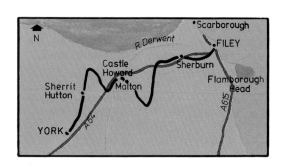

Length:	82 miles 132 kms
Status:	Regional route
From:	York
To:	Filey
Terrain:	Flat or gently rolling farmland finishing with sea cliffs
Maps:	OS Landranger 100, 101, 105
Access:	BR York. A64 from A1 BR Filey. Off A165 coast road.
Route Guides:	*The Centenary Way* (North Yorkshire County Council)
Information:	Highways Dept., County Hall, Northallerton, Yorks DL7 8AH

Creating this walk was one of the ways the North Yorkshire County Council (the old North Riding) chose to celebrate its own 100 years existence. It begins in the heart of the northern capital at the south transept door of York Minster and crosses the county in a north-easterly direction to the sea, passing through Areas of Outstanding Natural Beauty. Plenty of time is needed before setting out in order to visit the Minster, old city walls, gates, cobbled lanes and exceptional museums. The path which takes you out of the town follows the banks of the River Foss for an easy dozen miles to Sherrif Hutton where there is a ruined castle. Farm tracks and woodlands bring you next to Castle Howard where a short diversion will be needed to visit the famous stately home. Follies and other architectural features crown the surrounding hills. Further wooded trails and a stretch of arable country bring you to the valley of the River Derwent, the ruins of Kirkham Abbey and the bustling market town of Malton. Undulating wold country lies ahead for the next 20 miles, passing through pleasant villages like Thixendale and Sherburn. It is worth stopping between the two to explore the deserted medieval village of Wharram Percy. From Sherburn to the coast is another 15 miles. As it comes into view you have the striking outline of Flamborough Head to the south. To the north is Filey Bay, with the Brigg, a long rock reef, in the background. The trail meets up here with the Cleveland Way (q.v.) going north and the Wolds Way (q.v.) heading south.

York walls and Minster   *(Photo: Jarrold Publishing)*

CLEVELAND WAY

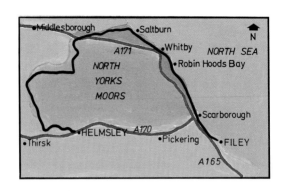

Length:	108 miles 172 kms
Status:	National trail
From:	Helmsley
To:	Filey
Terrain:	Moorland, farmland and sea coast. Quite tough stretches
Maps:	OS Landranger 93, 94, 99, 100, 101
Access:	BR Malton or Thirsk then bus. Off A170 from Thirsk BR Filey. A165 off A64 from York.
Route Guides:	*Cleveland Way* by I.Sampson (Aurum Press) *The Cleveland Way* by M.Boyes (Cicerone Press) *A Guide to the Cleveland Way* by R.Sale (Constable) *Cleveland Way* Companion by P. Hannon (Hillside)
Information:	North Yorks Moors National Park, The Old Vicarage, Helmsley, Yorks. YO6 5BP

A heady mixture of heather clad uplands, broad acres and sea coast. It was the second of Britain's national trails and takes a wide sweep through the North Yorks Moors National Park to meet the coast and follow the cliff line south. It should be taken that way if you want to get the hard work over first and finish with a more relaxing few days. Helmsley is a busy market town which is left via a steep wooded climb, descending through Nettle Dale. Leave time to see Rievaulx Abbey, magnificent even in ruin. Now over the Hambleton hills for views across the wide Vale of York. Landmarks are the white horse cut in the turf at Kilburn, and Sutton Bank, a formidable escarpment edge demanding a 1 in 4 climb. At Osmotherley begins the most strenuous part of the way, a succession of moors rising to a high point of 1,498 ft and taking in part of the legendary Lyke Wake Walk (q.v.). It drops eventually into Kildale and heads over Gisborough Moor to reach the sea at Saltburn. The coast path too has its share of gradients, surmounting the highest point on the English North Sea coast at Boulby, 666 ft above the waves. Fishing villages like Staithes, Runswick and Robin Hood's Bay occupy clefts in the cliffs. The great explorer Captain Cook learned his trade sailing out of them. At Whitby you needn't divert to see the cliff-top abbey because the route follows the 199 steps to the top. On the final stage the sea is on one hand, Fylingdale Moor on the other.

Whitby Abbey on Cleveland Way   *(Photo: Alex Wilson)*

COAST TO COAST WALK

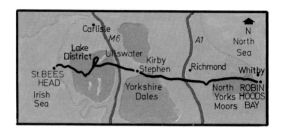

Length: 190 miles 304 kms

Status: Unofficial

From: St Bees Head

To: Robin Hood's Bay

Terrain: Mountains, high moorland and dales. Hard walking

Maps: OS Landranger 89, 90, 91, 92, 93, 94, 98, 99

Access: BR St Bees. M6 junction 40 and A66 or junction 35 and A590
BR Whitby and bus. A169 from York

Route Guides: *A Coast to Coast Walk* by A. Wainwright (Westmorland Gazette)

Information: Various national park and tourist offices.

Since the late Alfred Wainwright, fellsman extraordinary, devised this challenging walk it has outstripped many of the official trails in popularity. It crosses England from the Irish Sea to the North Sea, traversing three national parks in magnificent upland scenery. The 300 ft high red sandstone cliffs at St Bees Head mark the western end and it is better to start here to keep the prevailing weather at your back. The first day's walk brings you into the Lake District at Ennerdale Water, then the climbing starts in earnest, over High Stile or by a slightly lower route via Black Sail Pass. This leads into Borrowdale and on to Grasmere. There is an ascent of Helvellyn, 3,118 ft to follow, with a drop down the dizzying Striding Edge to the shores of Ullswater. Another day's march leaves Cumbria behind at Shap Fell and it is over the border to Kirkby Stephen and into the smoother but equally steep limestone slopes of the Yorkshire Dales. There is some easier going ahead following the river through Swaledale if you opt for one of Wainright's grudging 'low level alternatives'. This is after the Pennines watershed is reached on Nine Standards Rigg at 2,184 ft, but the climbing isn't over. There is a long series of switchback hills over the North Yorkshire Moors before the North Sea is sighted. The route follows the cliff line for the last few miles into Robin Hood's Bay, a fishing village clinging precariously to the cliffs. Wainwright expected those following his footsteps to be adept with map and compass.

Surrender Mine on the Coast to Coast   *(Photo: Alex Wilson)*

COED MORGANNWG WAY

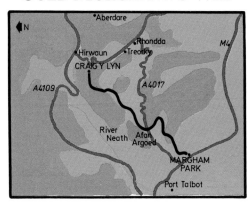

Length:	27 miles 43 kms
Status:	Regional route
From:	Craig y Llyn
To:	Margham Park
Terrain:	Steep forest tracks and hill ridges
Map:	OS Landranger 170
Access:	BR Rhondda. A4061 Hirwaum-Treorchy road BR Port Talbot and bus. M4 junction 40
Route Guides:	*Coed Morgannwg Way* leaflet (West Glamorgan County Council)
Information:	Environment & Highways Dept, West Glamorgan County Council, County Hall, Swansea SA1 3SN

A forest trail through South Wales which also has open hill-top stretches with excellent views. It breaks naturally in two for a week-end and there is a convenient half way area with a choice of accommodation at Afan Argoed. Paths are rough and gradients steep in places, but are generally well defined and firm. Some of them follow ancient trackways connecting Bronze and Iron Age settlements. Taken from the northern end the route begins from a popular beauty spot and follows the ridge between the valleys of the rivers Afan and Neath through plantations of sitka spruce, a hardy species which thrives at these windswept altitudes. The path quickly reaches a high spot at Pen-y-Cae, 1,830 ft where the Vale of Neath can be seen stretching down to the sea at Swansea. It then traverses a ridge between the Cymmer and Rheada Forests where the rocky crags are home to ravens and buzzards. A steep descent needing care takes the way into the Afan Valley, seen stretching dramatically below from the edge of the crags as the path twists and doubles back on itself. Panoramic views, sometimes across the Bristol Channel to Devon, stretch ahead as the trail passes through the Afan Argoed Country Park to Bryn, once a busy coal mining village, now silent. Twisting upwards again it plunges into mature deciduous woodlands where deer herds roam. The final descent is to the Margam Country Park close to Port Talbot. This was a private estate landscaped several centuries ago and makes a gentle contrast with which to finish.

Looking over the Afan Valley   *(Photo: West Glamorgan County Council)*

CORNWALL COAST PATH

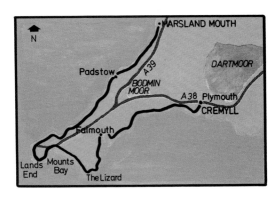

Length:	268 miles 431 kms
Status:	National trail
From:	Marsland Mouth
To:	Cremyll
Terrain:	Cliff top paths interspersed with coves. Moderate going
Maps:	OS Landranger 190, 200, 201, 203, 204
Access:	BR Barnstaple then bus. Off A39 via Morwenstow BR Plymouth then Cremyll ferry. Cars use Torpoint ferry
Route Guides:	*South West Way vols 1 & 2* by M.Collins (Cicerone) *South West Way vols 1-3* by various authors (Aurum Press)
Information:	South West Way Association, 1, Orchard Drive, Kingskerswell, Newton Abbot, Devon TQ12 5DG County Tourist Office, County Hall, Truro, Cornwall

Longest of the four sections which make up the South West Peninsula Coast Path. It follows the whole coastline of England's most sea-girt county, tracing every cove and headland from the northern boundary with Devon down to Land's End, then doubling back along the south coast. The north is the more rugged, being exposed to the full force of the Atlantic. The path begins near Bude and the first major landmark is Tintagel Castle, supposedly the seat of King Arthur. A ferry is needed to cross the broad estuary of the River Camel to reach Padstow and eventually Newquay (only big holiday resort on the north coast), via a string of golden surf beaches. With the exception of St Ives, noted artist colony, only tiny fishing villages punctuate the shoreline. Land's End is rather touristified, but Cape Cornwall just before it is unspoilt still. Heading east now, Mousehole and Newlyn are interesting old fishing ports on the way to Penzance, beyond which St Michael's Mount rises from the sea (accessible on foot at low tide). The Lizard, most southerly part of mainland Britain, is dotted with sandy coves. The path round it brings you to lovely Helford River (with Frenchman's Creek made famous by Daphne Du Maurier). Another ferry is needed from Falmouth to St Mawes, both guarded by huge Henry VIII castles. The rest of the trail is through a succession of beauty spots like Mevagissey, Fowey, Polperro, and Looe, linked by splendid cliff walks. Rame Head and Cawsand Cove make a perfect journey's end by Plymouth Sound.

Cawsand Bay, Cornwall

COTSWOLD WAY

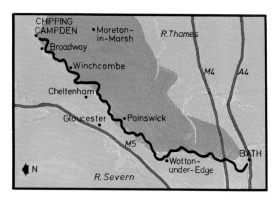

Length:	100 miles 161 kms
Status:	Regional route
From:	Chipping Campden
To:	Bath
Terrain:	A few climbs up steep scarp slopes but mainly gently undulating farmland and firm going
Maps:	OS Landranger 150, 151, 162, 163, 172
Access:	BR Moreton-in-Marsh then bus. Off A44 near Broadway BR Bath. M4 junction 18
Route Guides:	*The Cotswold Way* by K.Reynolds (Cicerone Press) *The Cotswold Way* by M.Richards (Penguin)
Information:	Cotswold Warden Service, Gloucestershire County Council, Shire Hall, Gloucester GL1 2TN

The Cotswolds is an area of rolling farmland famous for its stone villages and magnificent 'wool' churches, endowed when the prosperity of England was being founded on Cotswold sheep in Tudor times. It is mainly arable country now and although over 1,000 ft above sea level in places has little of the broken ground usually associated with upland areas, so the going is fairly easy. The Cotswolds stretch right across Gloucestershire and into much of Oxfordshire, but the Cotswold Way traces a line along the eastern escarpment with panoramic views across the Vale of Evesham, the Malvern Hills and the Severn Valley into Wales. Such are its attractions that it is being considered for up-grading to a national trail. Chipping Campden's old market hall is the starting point. First it climbs over Dover's Hill and drops into the showpiece village of Broadway. Ascending Shenbarrow Hill and Stumps Cross then leads to the ruins of Hailes Abbey and the historic jumbled streets of Winchcombe. Cleeve Cloud, highest part of the walk, comes next, then paths descend through a wooded stretch to Painswick, famous for its churchyard topiary. The way continues through hilly meadows and woods to Haresfield Beacon, then along the escarpment again before dropping down to cross the valley of the River Frome, climbing out of which it reaches the old market town of Wotton-under-Edge. The finish is in the centre of Regency Bath, beside the Abbey, Roman baths and Pump Room.

Chipping Campden, start of the Cotswold Way

CUMBRIA WAY

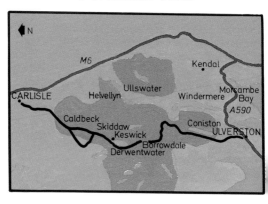

Length:	70 miles 112 kms
Status:	Unofficial
From:	Ulverston
To:	Carlisle
Terrain:	Moorland, lakeside and mountain passes, but despite nature of country none of it too difficult
Maps:	OS Landranger 85, 90, 97
Access:	BR Ulverston. A598 from M6 junction 36 BR Carlisle. M6 junction 43
Route Guides:	*The Cumbria Way* by J.Trevelyan (Dalesman Publishing)
Information:	Cumbria Tourist Board, Ashleigh, Holly Road, Windermere, Cumbria LA23 2AF

Unofficial perhaps, but this must be among the most glorious of English long distance treks, running through the heart of the incomparable Lake District. Despite being in the most mountainous part of England the Cumbria Way manages to take in much of the best scenery while sticking to mainly low level tracks. It skirts many lakes and goes over a few passes to give a wonderful feel of being in the mountains without venturing so high that there is a risk of walking being made unpleasant or impossible by low cloud. Anyone who wants to bag a few peaks need only leave extra time to divert. From Ulverston on the shores of Morcambe Bay the trail heads for its first big lake, Coniston Water, where excursions afloat will give the feet a rest. The path follows half the length of the northern shore to Coniston village before striking over the crags to the tourist honeypot at Tarn Hows. It then drops to Skelwith Bridge and the lesser known but more charming Elterwater. The Langdale Pikes tower above, but the path winds steadily to Dudgeon Ghyll and over Stake Pass into Borrowdale. Below lies Derwentwater with Keswick at its head. Skirting Skiddaw mountain the trail reaches the 2,000 ft contour, but there is an alternative lower level route. The northern Lakeland villages are less known and worth seeing. One of them is Caldbeck where (Do Ye Ken) John Peel is buried. The village takes its name from the River Calder which is kept company most of the way to the great Border bastion of Carlisle Castle.

Great Gable and Borrowdale   *(Photo: Alex Wilson)*

DALES WAY

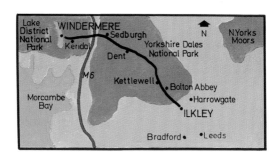

Length:	81 miles 130 kms
Status:	Unofficial
From:	Ilkley
To:	Bowness-on-Windermere
Terrain:	Limestone dales, river valleys, high moorland and crags
Maps:	OS Landranger 97, 98, 104
Access:	BR Ilkley. On A65 Leeds-Skipton road BR Bowness. A59 from M6 junction 36
Route Guides:	*The Dales Way* by C.Speakman (Dalesman Publications) *Dales Way Companion* by P.Hannan (Hillside Publications) *Dales Way Route Guide* by Gemmell & Speakman (Stile Publications)
Information:	West Riding Area Ramblers' Association, Cookridge Ave, Cookridge, Leeds 16 Tourist Office, Station Rd, Ilkley, W. Yorks.

An exciting trail which links two national parks, both uplands of great beauty but different character. It leaves the dense conurbations of West Yorkshire to traverse the limestone dales, cross the Pennines and terminate by the banks of Windermere in the Lake District. Appropriately it starts by crossing Ilkley Moor (b'aht 'at) and there are link paths to the start from Leeds, Bradford and Harrogate. The route follows the major Yorkshire Dales rivers, so some sections are along level riverside paths, the steep bits coming as you get nearer the source and cross from the head of one dale to another. Wharfdale is the first, with the river flowing past the ruins of Bolton Abbey. It passes the lovely villages of Grassington and Kettlewell before the source is found on Camm Fell. Then it drops into Dentdale, following the river through Dent and Sebergh with the Howgill fells dominating the skyline. The dales of the limestone country are left behind and the more broken crags and fells of Lakeland lie ahead, with some remote stretches over Lambrigg Fell and Black Moss. A notable sight hereabouts is the Ribblehead viaduct of the Settle-Carlisle railway. You have to pass over the M6, but that is the only intrusion on the peace in many miles. The walk has a perfect climax with the Lake District hills crowning the horizon. When you drop through the bustling streets of Bowness to the Windermere shore journey's end is rewarded with one of the most breathtaking views in England.

In the Yorkshire dales   *(Photo: Ian Howard)*

DORSET COAST PATH

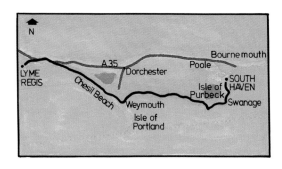

Length:	72 miles 116kms
Status:	National trail
From:	Lyme Regis
To:	South Haven
Terrain:	Smooth downland clifftops, but some very stiff climbs
Maps:	OS Landranger 193, 194, 195
Access:	BR Axminster and bus. Turning off A35 BR Poole or Bournemouth then bus and ferry. Car ferry from Sandbanks or A351 via Wareham
Route Guides:	*South West Way vol 2* by M.Collins (Cicerone Press) *South West Way vol 4* by R. Tarr (Aurum Press)
Information:	South West Way Association, 1, Orchard Drive, Kingskerswell, Newton Abbot, Devon TQ12 5DG Dorset Information Office, County Hall, Dorchester

First or last of the four sections of the 560 mile long South West Peninsula Coast Path. It is quite different to the others, the coastline less tortured, the hills more

smoothly rounded and it passes through some of the
best country of Thomas Hardy's Wessex. In the west it
begins at Lyme Regis harbour on the Cobb (ancient
stone pier), made famous by Jane Austen and others.
The first target ahead is Golden Cap, highest cliff on
the English Channel coast. Dropping down its eastern
slope brings you to charming Chideock and another
climb to Thorncombe Beacon before an easy drop into
West Bay, the harbour for Bridport where they made
rope for sailing ships. At Burton Bradstock the coastal
scenery changes and is dominated by the seven mile
long Chesil Bank, the biggest shingle beach in Europe
running all the way to Portland Bill, but much too
punishing to walk. Behind it paths meander through
salt marshes to lovely Abbotsbury whose medieval
swannery and other antiquities are worth stopping for.
Following the Fleet (a lake behind Chesil Bank) brings
you to Weymouth's wide, sandy bay. George III's
equestrian figure cut in the chalk hillside leads you out
of the town and over some fine stretches of rolling
cliff to Lulworth Cove, an amazing natural harbour. St
Aldhelm's Head with its hermit's chapel signals the
final section, dropping into Swanage by Durlston
Head, then over Ballard Down to Studland village and
a last mile along smooth, firm sand to the mouth of
Poole Harbour.

Abbotsbury on the Dorset Coast Path

EAST RIDING HERITAGE WALK

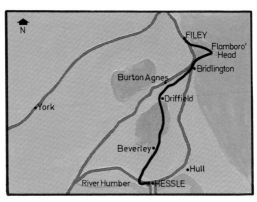

Length:	80 miles 128 kms
Status:	Regional route
From:	Hessle
To:	Filey
Terrain:	Undulating wolds, flat farmland and fairly steep cliffs
Maps:	OS Landranger 101, 106
Access:	BR Hessle. A63 from north or via Humber Bridge from south BR Filey. Turning off A64 from York
Route Guides:	Set of leaflets (Humberside County Council)
Information:	Humberside County Council, Countryside Section, County Hall, Beverley HU7 9XA

This trail celebrates the wide acres of the old East Riding of Yorkshire which lost its identity in 1974. Even more than the other two 'ridings' it was a county of sharp contrasts and the trail takes them all in. It was devised as a series of four separate but joined walks, each with its own name and each roughly 20 miles long. The first part, called the Beverley 20, shares a

start with the Wolds Way (q.v.) by the Humber road
bridge at Hessle, an outlier of Hull. It follows the
mudflats of the Humber westwards before turning
inland to make a meandering north-easterly course
along tracks that are moderately up and down, to reach
Beverley, a town with a fine ancient Minster. Part two,
the Hutton Hike, follows the course of the River Hull
out of Beverley before striking off over fens and dykes
to reach Riverhead and the busy market town of
Driffield. From here the third section, the Rudston
Roam, provides another change of mood by crossing
the wolds to Burton Agnes and following a Roman
road to the ancient monolith at Rudston. The day ends
at the sea, dropping into Bridlington, a busy fishing
harbour and popular seaside resort and a good place to
relax before the more demanding walk ahead in the
last part. This is the Headland Walk which strikes
northwards, up and down the high chalk cliffs to
Flamborough Head, the most prominent headland on
the long Yorkshire coast. After another ten miles of
breezy cliff-top the route ends in Filey where it meets
the Cleveland Way and Wolds Way (q.v.).

Silex Bay, Flamborough   *(Photo: Humberside County Council)*

ESSEX WAY

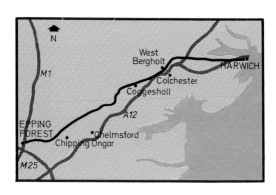

Length:	81 miles 130 kms
Status:	Regional route
From:	Epping Forest
To:	Harwich
Terrain:	Woodland paths, cornfields and saltings, almost all flat
Maps:	OS Landranger 167, 168, 169
Access:	BR Epping. From M11/M25 interchange BR Harwich. A120 from A12 Colchester
Route Guides:	*Essex Way* by Matthews & Bitten (F.Matthews)
Information:	Essex County Council, County Hall, Chelmsford CM1 1LX

This trail heads for the sea by non-touristy routes and the walker will be rewarded by some profound redisoveries of rural peace. It is soon evident why the area inspired Constable and other painters. The start is in Epping Forest, preserved for the public by a pioneering conservation battle as long ago as 1878. This is commemorated in the Epping Forest Centenary Walk from Manor Park tube station which will add another 15 miles to the journey for anyone who wants to start the trail from London. The 6,000 acres of forest make a fine start to the Essex Way. Emerging into open country the trail reaches Chipping Ongar, near which is the only wooden Saxon church in England. About the mid-way mark the half timbered houses of Coggeshall, built by wealthy cloth merchants, are ample reason to dawdle. The way now enters Constable country, following the River Colne to West Bergholt where the painter was born. It passes through Dedham Vale where he painted many of his famous pictures, locations of which can still be recognised. In Dedham village lived another famous artist, Sir Alfred Munnings, and his house with a large collection of paintings can be visited. The last section is along the estuary of the River Stour. Not long ago the villages it passes through, like Mistley and Manningtree, were busy with the traffic of Thames sailing barges. Some can still be seen surviving as yachts, but most of the enjoyment of following the sea wall and marshes will be in watching the prolific bird life.

Flatford Mill in Constable country (*Photo: Ian Howard*)

GLENDOWER'S WAY

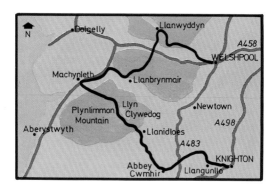

Length:	125 miles 200 kms
Status:	National trail designate
From:	Knighton
To:	Welshpool
Terrain:	Varied, mainly hill country with some remote moorland
Maps:	OS Landranger 125, 126, 135, 136, 148
Access:	BR Knighton. A488 Shrewbury-Llandidrod Wells road BR Welshpool. A458 from Shrewbury
Route Guides:	Set of 16 leaflets (Powys County Council)
Information:	Planning Dept, Powys County Council, County Hall, Llandrindod Wells LD1 5LG

In Welsh it is Fford Glyndwr, a theme walk to celebrate the national hero Owen Glendower who almost succeeded in driving the English out. It visits many sites associated with his life and struggles, describing a huge arc through central Wales. At both ends it connects with Offa's Dyke (q.v.). From the clock tower in Knighton the path runs westwards over

Bailey Hill to Llangunllo, a gentle introduction to the
upland country ahead. Striking north to skirt Beacon
Hill and dropping into the Teme Valley it enters
typical Welsh hill farming country with magnificent
views. The way reaches its most southerly point at
Abbey Cwmhir after a fine edge walk above Bachell
Brook. Forest paths provide the route for the next
dozen miles as it heads north west to Llanidloes. The
views then become more exciting as the way climbs
out of the Severn valley and along the banks of Llyn
Clywedog, a large reservoir and wildlife haven. From
here there is a climb over the foothills of the
Plynlimmon range to reach Machynlleth, furthest west
point, where Glendower was crowned Prince of
Wales. It is a fine town with many historic buildings.
Heading now north-east the trail makes several sharp
climbs to Cemmaes Road at the confluence of the
rivers Dovey and Tywyn. A wild stretch lies ahead
between Llanbrynmair and Llangadfan with few
opportunities for shelter and refreshment. The final
stages become easier through lower lying farmland,
until the red towers of Powys Castle signal the finish.

Welsh hills near Glendower's Way

GREENSAND RIDGE WALK

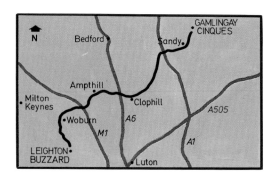

Length:	40 miles 64 kms
Status:	Regional route
From:	Leighton Buzzard
To:	Gamlingay Cinques
Terrain:	Level woods and fields with mildly steep patches of heath
Maps:	OS Landranger 153, 165
Access:	BR Leighton Buzzard. M1 junction 12 BR Sandy and bus. Minor roads from A1
Route Guides:	Leaflet from Bedfordshire County Council
Information:	Leisure Services Dept., County Hall, Bedford MK42 9AP

The ridge of green sandstone that bisects Bedfordshire makes a handy trail across one of England's smaller counties. The well-drained soil makes it usually dry underfoot. This is the country John Bunyan knew. It is more wooded than in his day and home to a diversity of flora and fauna, not least to the feral deer which are quite common. From the centre of Leighton Buzzard the towpath of the Grand Union Canal provides the first part of the trail, leading to a series of woods, some modern plantations, some ancient oak. These bring the trail to the 3,000 acre parklands of Woburn Abbey which it crosses. This home of the Dukes of Bedford has plenty of attractions and facilities to linger over. The village of Woburn has a fine Georgian centre and its church is one of many on the trail built of the distinctive greensand stone. Further on at Ampthill Park is a cross marking the spot where Henry VIII kept Katharine of Aragon imprisoned in the now demolished castle. Jacobean Houghton House, the next prominent site, is believed to be the original of 'House Beautiful' in Pilgrim's Progress. Maulden Wood beyond is a Site of Special Scientific Interest. An impressive double avenue of trees at Highland Farm marks a change of scenery for more open, fertile farmland which continues to Sandy where, on the hill, Caesar's Camp may have been a Roman fort and the walk itself now follows a Roman road. The finish is at the top of Tetworth Hill, just outside the village of Gamlingay Cinques.

Greesand Ridge Walk near Sandy   *(Photo: Grant Wilson)*

GREENSAND WAY

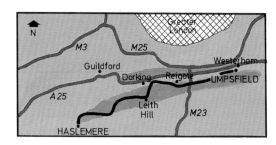

Length:	55 miles 88 kms
Status:	Regional route
From:	Haslemere
To:	Limpsfield
Terrain:	Heath and wooded hills, some steep climbs. Firm and dry
Maps:	OS Landranger 186, 187
Access:	BR Haslemere. A286 off A3 BR Oxted. A25 from M25 junction 6
Route Guides:	*The Greensand Way in Surrey* (Surrey County Council)
Information:	Public Relations Unit, Surrey County Council, County Hall, Kingston-on-Thames KT1 2DN

Between the North and South Downs a belt of greensand, an older sedimentary rock than chalk, throws another ridge across the south-east corner of England. Walking along it gives a bird's-eye view of leafy Surrey. The ridge continues through Kent for another 50 miles but the two sections have yet to be integrated into one long trail. The Surrey way begins in High Street, Haslemere, a pleasant country town, and first crosses Hundred Common, an extensive area of National Trust land. This leads to the first climb, up the ridge to Gibbet Hill. Then the path drops down to the Devil's Punchbowl, a bracken covered coombe, and follows the old Portsmouth stage coach road to Thursley's Saxon church. After this are more ups and downs through Witeley Park and across the Hambledon hills to Hascombe. After the Winkworth Arboretum the way enters a 12 mile stretch generally reckoned the finest on the route and including 4,000 acres of heathland called Hurstwood. Then Reynard's Hill, Pitch Hill and Holmbury Hill which has a prehistoric fort. Finally comes Leith Hill, 965 ft, highest point in Surrey, albeit artificially elevated by the landowner in 1766 to make sure his was top. Heading northwards into the Tillingbourne valley opens up different scenery with clear streams and little waterfalls, before turning east again for Dorking. The heights are regained over Reigate Common which has a restored windmill and the last section is over Tilburstow Hill to Tandridge where the church has a 1,000 year old yew.

Descending Leith Hill on the Surrey greensand

HEART OF ENGLAND WAY

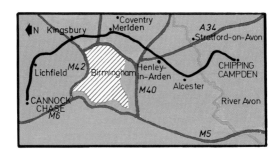

Length:	80 miles 128 kms
Status:	Regional route
From:	Cannock Chase
To:	Chipping Campden
Terrain:	Varied, but mostly flat and well wooded with farm and riverside paths
Maps:	OS Landranger 127, 128, 139, 150, 151
Access:	BR Stafford, then bus. M6 junction 12 BR Moreton-in-Marsh and bus. 'B' roads from A34
Route Guides:	*Heart of England Way* by J.Watts (Thornhill Press) *Heart of England Way* by J.Roberts (Walkways)
Information:	Heart of England Way Association, 50 George Rd, Water Orton, Birmingham B46 1PE

Through the central counties of the English Midlands, starting in Staffordshire, crossing Warwickshire and ending in Gloucestershire. Cannock Chase where it starts was once a royal forest and is now a large area of open heath. From it the route heads for Lichfield

Cathedral whose triple spires act as a landmark most of the way. The town produced Samuel Johnson and David Garrick and there is a museum in the former's birthplace. Open farmland paths lead to Drayton Manor Park, once the home of Sir Robert Peel who founded the modern police force. Further on is Kingsbury Country Park, a 400 acre habitat for large numbers of water fowl. Ways well lined with hedgerows and small woods lead to Meriden, the village which claims to be the geographical centre of England. It marks the begining of the leafy Arden country immortalised by Shakespeare. There are many associations with the Bard in the well kept villages around and Stratford-on-Avon is only a short diversion off the route. Baddesley Clinton Hall on the path to Henley-in-Arden is the finest preserved moated medieval manor house in the country. A working water mill makes an interesting stop before Alcester where the entire village is a conservation area. Ragley Hall, stately home of the Marquess of Hertford, is only a mile off the track. Willow-lined paths along the banks of the River Avon bring the route eventually to the northern slopes of the Costwold Hills and the mellow stone buildings of Chipping Campden.

Hidcote Gardens, a halt on the Heart of England Way

HEREWARD WAY

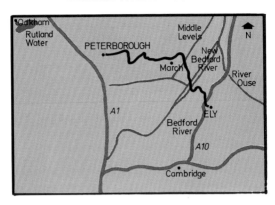

Length:	43 miles 68 kms
Status:	Regional route
From:	Peterborough
To:	Ely
Terrain:	Flat fenland
Maps:	OS Landranger 141, 142, 143, 144
Access:	BR Peterbrough. Just off A1
	BR Ely. A10 from Cambridge
Route Guides:	*The Hereward Way* by T.Noyes
	(Ramblers' Association)
Information:	Rural Management Dept,
	Cambridgeshire County Council,
	Shire Hall, Cambridge CB3 0AP

Officially there are 43 miles of this trail. Unofficially there are 102 miles running from Oakham in Leicestershire where it links up with the Viking Way (q.v.) to Thetford in Norfolk at the start of the Peddars Way (q.v.) Only the official part is fully waymarked. Despite having a novel about him by Charles Kingsley the Saxon baron Hereward the Wake is a forgotten hero, but for eight years he defied William the Conqueror, leading his guerilla army from watery hideouts among the fens which the Normans could never penetrate. In those days it was all deep marsh and the 'island' place names which appear on the modern map were islands in fact. It has been drained and cultivated since 1600 when the Duke of Bedford called in Dutch engineers. The result is a unique fenland landscape with the most low lying land in Britain, which makes this trek across Cambridgeshire different to any other. The official start is close to Peterborough Cathedral and follows the willow-lined banks of the River Nene, past the remains of a Saxon village at Flag Fen. The track is often along the tops of raised embankments built to keep the land from flooding again and this gives a good commanding view of the country. In Hereward's day one of the few ways of getting from island to island in this territory was on stilts. One such island was Whittersley, still a sleepy village, from which the line of a Roman road takes the way to March. Ely at the end of the trail is perhaps England's least well known cathedral city.

Fen country on Hereward Way   *(Photo: Cambridgeshire County Council)*

IMBER RANGE PERIMETER PATH

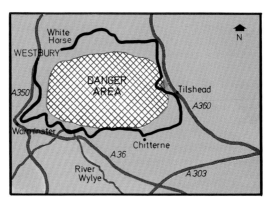

Length:	30 miles 48 kms
Status:	Regional route
From:	Westbury
To:	Westbury (circular)
Terrain:	Chalk downland. Dry, firm going. Easy climbs
Map:	OS Landranger 184
Access:	BR Westbury. A350 from M4 junction 17
Route Guides:	*Imber Range Perimeter Path* leaflet (Wilts County Council)
Information:	Dept of Planning, Wiltshire County Council, County Hall, Trowbridge, Wilts BA14 8JD

A walk round the edge of the Forbidden Land. It circumnavigates the army's largest live firing range in the south of England. For 50 years an area of Salisbury Plain ten miles long and five miles wide has been occupied by the army and public access is very limited. But there are compensations. Army occupation keeps developers out so the traditional landscape is untouched. For getting to know something of Salisbury Plain this circular trail is fine, but don't stray off the waymarked route, especially if there are red flags flying. Westbury, suggested here as a possible starting point, has one of those Wiltshire specialities, a white horse cut in the hillside in 1778. Moving off in a clockwise direction the path climbs to Bratton Camp, an Iron Age hill fort from whose ramparts there is a wide view over Wiltshire and Somerset. The next stop is the village of Edington where King Alfred defeated the Danes. A by-way which takes the trail from here over Coulston Hill and Littleton Down is part of the old Salisbury to Bath stage coach road. At Gore Cross the route swings south marching among the tumuli on Horse Down till it drops into Tilshead village. Turning west it goes over Copehill Down to Chitterne, climbs Breakheart Hill and heads for more hill forts on Scratchbury and Battlesbury Hills which look over the Wylye valley. By-passing the town of Warminster it climbs Cradle Hill which has a reputation for UFO sightings. Half a dozen miles from here completes the circuit to Westbury.

Westbury white horse, Wiltshire

ISLE OF WIGHT COAST PATH

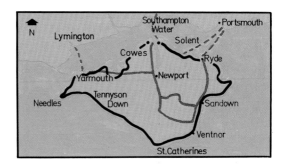

Length:	67 miles 108 kms
Status:	Regional route
From:	Any ferry point on island
To:	Return to same point
Terrain:	Mixture of cliff paths, chalk downland and level shore
Maps:	OS Landranger 196 or Outdoor Leisure 29
Access:	Car and passenger ferries Lymington-Yarmouth, Southampton-Cowes, Portsmouth-Fishbourne and passenger only Portsmouth-Ryde. All served by BR mainland stations
Route Guides:	*The Isle of Wight Coast Path* by A.Charles (Thornhill) *The Isle of Wight Coast Path* by J.Merrill (JNM Publications)
Information:	Countryside Management Services, I.O.W. County Council, Newport, Isle of Wight PO30 1UD

There is something romantic about circumnavigating an island, even a populated one. This path traces the whole coastline and as public transport on the island is very good, and there are also six criss-crossing link trails, walkers can begin and finish where they like, or even tackle the sections from a single overnight base. From any of the ferry ports the path starts level, overlooking the Solent with its busy shipping. Queen Victoria's Osborne House, Carisbrooke Castle and the yachting mecca at Cowes (via free ferry across the Medina river) are among the early points of interest. Alum Bay with its remarkable coloured sands is at the western end, marked at the seaward extremity by the famous row of chalk stacks called The Needles. To look down on them the path climbs higher and enters smooth downland, part of it called Tennyson Down because the Victorian Poet Laureate lived here. The line along the southern shore looks out on the English Channel and follows an old military road built in the mid 19th century to guard against French invasion and not opened to public use till 100 years later. After descending deep down Blackgang Chine the route reaches the southern tip at St Catherine's lighthouse. Then the mood changes and it passes by a succession of coves and sandy beaches round Ventnor, Shanklin and Sandown to reach the easterly tip at Bembridge. Here the landscape is salt marsh and the return western leg along the Solent shore offers an easy level finish all the way.

The Needles from the Isle of Wight Coast Path

KENNET & AVON CANAL PATH

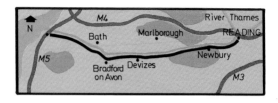

Length:	86 miles 138 kms
Status:	Regional route designate
From:	Reading
To:	Bristol
Terrain:	Flat tow path. Good surface, mostly dry
Maps:	OS Landranger 172, 173, 174, 175
Access:	BR Reading General. M4 junction 10 or 11 BR Bristol Temple Meads. M4 junction 19

Route Guides: *Exploring the Kennet & Avon Canal* by N.Vile (Countryside)

Information: No single source yet available

Walks along canals have not been generally included in this book because most have right of way along the tow path and walkers need little help following them. An exception has been been made of the Kennet & Avon, firstly because it is one of the longest and most interesting and secondly because there is a scheme afoot by Berkshire County Council and other authorities to turn it into a long distance trail for disabled people, taking advantage of the firm and level nature of the path. Transport history is marked by

attempts to find a better way west - the ancient
Ridgeway (q.v.), the Old Bath Road, the Kennet &
Avon Canal completed by Rennie in 1810, the Great
Western Railway which killed it, and finally the M4,
all occupying the same broad corridor across the
country. The grand design of the canal was to link the
ports of London and Bristol, leaving the Thames at
Reading and following the valley of the River Kennet.
After Theale, nine miles from the start, the vistas are
wide and airy with the Berkshire Downs in view to the
north. Beyond Hungerford lies Savernake Forest and
on the right day the Crofton beam engine may in
operation. It is one of the oldest relics of the steam age
still working, built to feed the canal with water. On the
approach to Devizes is a remarkable staircase of 16
locks and at Great Bedwyn a lugubrious collection of
rare tombstones. Bradford-on-Avon is worth exploring
and the attractions of Bath, through which the canal
passes, need no recommendation.

Kennet & Avon canal at Bathampton

KING ALFRED'S WAY

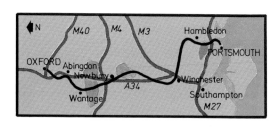

Length:	108 miles 172 kms
Status:	Unofficial
From:	Portsmouth
To:	Oxford
Terrain:	River valleys, chalk downs and field paths. Moderate climbs
Maps:	OS Landranger 164, 174, 185, 196
Access:	BR Portsmouth Harbour. M27 junction 12 BR Oxford. From A34 or M40 to city centre
Route Guides:	*King Alfred's Way* by L.Main (Thornhill Press)
Information:	Southern Tourist Board, Old Town Hall, Eastleigh, Hants Thames & Chilterns Tourist Board, Abingdon, OX14 4DE

He who burned the cakes also freed his people, brought light and learning to the Dark Ages and a lot else. But don't take it as a walking history lesson unless you want to. It has a variety of beautiful country and interesting things to see. The start at the Royal Dockyard in Portsmouth marks the fact that

Alfred founded the English navy. Naturally none of his ships survive, but there is the Tudor *Mary Rose*, the Georgian *Victory* and the Victorian *Warrior* to see. History of a different sort was made at Hambledon, first village to the north. It was the birthplace of the game of cricket. Its paths lead to Winchester which was Alfred's capital. King Arthur was there first though and the legendary Round Table of his knights is in the Great Hall. A switchback of chalk downs continues through Hampshire and into Berkshire. Alfred may have been the bloke who settled most of the county boundaries we know to-day. After crossing the River Kennet at Newbury and passing Donnington Castle a climb up the Berkshire Downs leads through noted racehorse training country round Lambourne. On the summit the route crosses the Ridgeway (q.v.) and drops down to Alfred's birthplace at Wantage, marked by a statue in the market place. The River Thames is reached at Abingdon and Oxford is sighted from the low hills ahead. Some say Alfred may have founded Oxford University in 872 AD. In the city's Ashmolean Museum is one of his royal jewels, found a 1,000 years after he lost it when a fugitive in the Somerset marshes.

King Alfred in Wantage market place

LELAND TRAIL

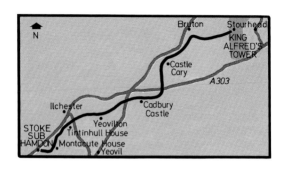

Length:	28 miles 44 kms
Status:	Regional route
From:	Stourhead
To:	Stoke sub Hambdon
Terrain:	Low laying pasture and arable land with commanding hills
Maps:	OS Landranger 183, 193
Access:	BR Bruton and bus. Off A303 at Mere BR Yeovil and bus. Off A303 near Ilchester
Route Guides:	*Leland Trail* wallet with cards (South Somerset District Council)
Information:	Leisure & Arts Dept., South Somerset District Council, Bryanston Way, Yeovil

Somerset's imaginative contribution to the network of recreational routes. It takes the walker across lush green dairy country. The name comes from John Leland, royal librarian to Henry VIII who sometime between 1535 and 1543 made a journey through Somerset. Luckily he left a detailed account, so it has been possible to follow closely in his footsteps. Leland recorded the buildings, local traditions and character of the countryside as he went and it is fascinating to see what has endured and what has changed 450 years later. The starting point, 100 yards from the Wiltshire border, is the 160 ft high King Alfred's Tower marking the spot where Alfred the Great organised resistance to the Danes. It stands on Kingsettle Hill on the edge of the Stourhead estate which has one of the most famous landscaped gardens in England. A ridge top path leads to Castle Cary which has many antiquities apart from its castle. Cadbury Castle on the next stretch is associated with legends of King Arthur, but rather more tangible modern warriors will be found at the Royal Naval Air Service Museum nearby. Just beyond Ilchester is Tintinhull House which was there when Leland made the journey. He was just a little too early to see Montacute House, an outstanding Elizabethan manor now splendidly restored. From it a Roman road leads to St Michael's Mount, a Norman motte and bailey castle completed in 1086. One more hill remains, Ham Hill where you can look back for a panoramic view over the whole trail.

Alfred's Tower, start of the Leland Trail

LONDON COUNTRYWAY

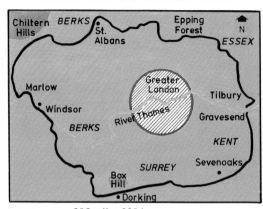

Length:	205 miles 330 kms
Status:	Unofficial
From:	Any point on route
To:	Return to start
Terrain:	Mixture of fields, woods, riverside paths and moderate hills
Maps:	OS Landranger 165, 166, 167, 175, 177, 186, 187, 188
Access:	Numerous BR commuter stations close to route Any arterial roads out of London
Route Guides:	*A London Countryway* by K.Chesterton (Constable)
Information:	Long Distance Walkers Association, 7, Ford Drive, Yarnfield, Stone, Staffs ST15 0RP

Notable because it completely encircles London like a walkers' version of the M25. Though in places no more than a dozen miles from the centre of the capital, and never more than 30 miles away, it passes through country as quiet and unfrequented as any in the deep shires. In an area with such good public transport it is an ideal trail for tackling in day or week-end sections.

For the sake of starting somewhere the guide book description begins at Box Hill, the popular Surrey beauty spot, and travels clockwise through Surrey, Berks, Bucks, Herts, Essex and Kent. Crossing the Surrey heathlands and commons the trail meets up with the Wey Canal, follows it to West Byfleet and over Chobham Common to Windsor Great Park and Virginia Water. Here it joins the Thames which it follows to Marlow where the beech woods mark the start of the Chiltern Hills. Before these are tackled (the steepest part of the course) there are diversions such as Wycombe House, home of the infamous 18th century Hell Fire Club. Over the Chilterns is St Albans with its cathedral and Roman ruins. Passing through Hertfordshire via Waltham Abbey brings the trail to Epping Forest, then another change of mood as the way winds through the Essex marshes to Tilbury. There is a ferry crossing over the Thames here to reach Gravesend on the Kent shore in order to complete the southern part of the circuit over the North Downs. There is so much to stop and see on the way that it is worth planning to do this trail in short stages over a long period.

Box Hill, Surrey on the London Countryway

LYKE WAKE WALK

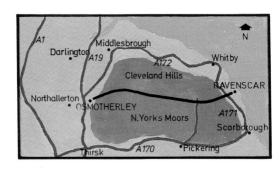

Length:	40 miles 64 kms
Status:	Unofficial
From:	Osmotherly
To:	Ravenscar
Terrain:	Remote high moorland. Very tough going
Maps:	OS Landranger 93, 94, 99, 100
Access:	BR Northalleton and bus. Off A19 BR Scarborugh and bus. A168 coast road
Route Guides:	*Lyke Wake Walk* by B.Cowley (Dalesman Publishing)
Information:	North Yorkshire Moors National Park, The Old Vicarage, Bondgate, Helmsley, North Yorkshire YO6 5BP Lyke Wake Club, Goulton Grange, Swainby, Northallerton

Something of a cult walk with northern ramblers, crossing the wildest and highest part of the North Yorkshire Moors till they meet the sea cliffs north of Scarborough. It is over much boggy and rough terrain, goes through no villages and crosses few roads. The done thing is to finish the whole 40 miles inside 24

hours which qualifies successful candidates for
membership of the slightly zany Lyke Wake Club. The
walk across this virtual wilderness was thought of 40
years ago by farmer Bill Cowley. Then it was
practically trackless, deep in heather and bracken and
needing a compass course to follow. As a result of the
popularity which developed after he had written about
it the walk has become well marked with tracks made
by thousands of pairs of boots. Nevertheless bad
weather and poor visibility can still trap the unwary
and there is no signposting on the open moors.
Breaking it into stages over two or three days is not
easy because of the remoteness from accommodation
and refreshment. For this reason an alternative 'Lyke
Wake Walk Way' has been devised, taking in the best
features of the original route but staying nearer to
human habitation. Large walking parties and challenge
events are having to be discouraged from using the
original route because of the land erosion problems
caused. 'Lyke Wake' is the title of an ancient
Yorkshire funeral dirge. Adopting it as the name of the
walk appealed to the sense of humour of the original
pioneers.

Fylingdale Moor near the end of the Lyke Wake   *(Photo: Alex Wilson)*

NENE WAY

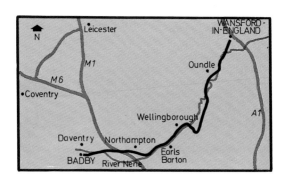

Length:	71 miles 113 kms
Status:	Regional route
From:	Badby
To:	Wansford-in-England
Terrain:	Riverside paths, woods & fields. Few slopes, can be muddy
Maps:	OS Landranger 152
Access:	BR Northampton and bus. M1 junction 16 towards Daventry BR Peterborough & bus. Junction of A1 and A47
Route Guides:	*Nene Way* set of leaflets (Northamptonshire County Council)
Information:	County Leisure Officer, 27 Guildhall Rd, Northampton

Northamptonshire is not the county the motorist sees, thick with lorries thundering up the M1. It is still one of the rolling shires, home of famous hunts like the Pytchley and the countryside which inspired its native poet John Clare. Its main river is the Nene which the trail follows from the source near the bluebell woods of Badby until it crosses into Cambridgeshire. Look

out on the first section for the ridge and furrow
patterns made by medieval open field systems and one
of the largest village greens in England at Nether
Heyford. A building in Weedon was put up as a hiding
place for George III in case Napoleon ever invaded.
Beyond Northampton the village of Earls Barton has a
rare Saxon church spire, one of the first ever built in
stone. The river skirts Wellingborough, a busy town
which made its Victorian wealth in the boot industry,
but which has pleasant older corners. Many of the
churches on the route are impressive, like the one at
Higham Ferrers, and Oundle with its famous public
school is also worth exploring. On the final section
there is Ashton, a model village built by one of the
Rothschilds, now noted for the annual World Conker
Championships held on the village green. At this end
of the route are also some of the stations of the Nene
Valley Steam Railway which runs to Peterborough.
Wansford-in-England may seem an odd place-name to
finish at. Needless to say there is a local legend about
how the village came to be called that, but walkers
may please themselves whether they believe it!

Never too young for the Nene Way

NORTH DOWNS WAY

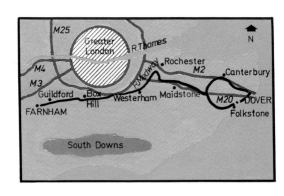

Length:	141 miles 227 kms
Status:	National trail
From:	Farnham, Surrey
To:	Dover, Kent
Terrain:	Varied, woods and farmland. Fairly easy walking
Maps:	OS Landranger 178, 179, 186, 187, 188, 189
Access:	BR Farnham. A287 from M3 junction 5 BR Dover. M2 and A2
Route Guides:	*North Downs Way* by N. Curtis (Aurum Press) *Guide to the Pilgrims Way & North Downs Way* by C.J.Wright (Constable) *Discovering the North Downs Way* (Shire Publications)
Information:	South East England Tourist Board, 1 Warwick Park, Tunbridge Wells TN1 1NH

The North Downs dominate the countryside south of London, across the counties of Kent and Surrey. Historically it always was an important highway, keeping early travellers on the drier high ground.

Some believe its alignment follows closely that of a much longer ancient Pilgrims' Way from Winchester to Canterbury though there is a lot of doubt about this. Nevertheless it runs the length of two Areas of Outstanding Natural Beauty and despite being frequently pierced by modern roads radiating from the capital its rural peace is quickly regained. The start is along sandy heathlands before the first climb to the southern escarpment of the downs after skirting the Hog's Back near Guildford. Famous National Trust houses like Polesdon Lacy and Knole are a feature of this walk. The steepest climb is up the popular Box Hill before crossing the Kent border and heading for Westerham. Sir Winston Churchill's house at Chartwell (open to the public) is close by. The scenery changes as the trail reaches the River Medway which is kept close company nearly to its confluence with the Thames. Then the trail turns south-east to pass through the orchard landscape which gave Kent the title of the Garden of England. Blossom time in spring sees it at its best. There is an optional diversion at the end to take in Canterbury and its cathedral. This adds about ten miles to the total. The shorter route reaches the sea near Folkstone and goes along the white cliffs to Dover Castle.

North Downs near Reigate Common, Surrey

OFFA'S DYKE PATH

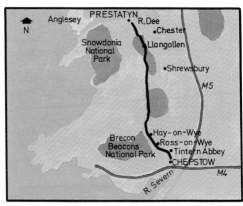

Length:	168 miles 270 kms
Status:	National trail
From:	Chepstow
To:	Prestatyn
Terrain:	Varied, preponderence of hilly country, some strenuous
Maps:	OS Landranger 117, 117, 126, 137, 148, 161, 162
Access:	BR Chepstow. M4, junction 22 BR Prestatyn. A548 North Wales coast road from Chester
Route Guides:	*Offa's Dyke Path 2 vols* by Kay & Richards (Aurum Press)
Information:	Offa's Dyke Association, Old Primary School, West St, Knighton, Powys LD7 1EW

Offa, King of Mercia built the dyke around 790AD, perhaps as a fortified boundary against the Welsh, but archaeologists aren't too sure. At any rate there it is, a great ditch and bank, 25 feet high in places, running along the English-Welsh border from the Severn to the Dee. The path follows alongside 80 miles of it that survive and for the rest takes a probable route through the Border Marches with their mighty castles and ruins of long silent abbeys. A deceptively easy start follows the gentle River Wye past Chepstow Castle and Tintern Abbey. At Monmouth the going gets stiffer as path and dyke climb into the Black Mountains to a summit at Hay Bluff, 2,220 ft. Below is Hay-on-Wye, famous for its second hand bookshops. A gentler stretch of woods and low hills leads to Knighton, but the hardest part is to come when the dyke switchbacks up and down the border hills. Between here and Montgomery some of the best bits of the dyke can be seen running ahead over the hills for mile after mile. There is then level walking for a stretch around Welshpool as the route follows the Shropshire Union canal. A few modest gradients after this lead to Chirk Castle and Llangollen where walkers have the option of an alternative route over Telford's famous Pontcysyllte Viaduct carrying the Llangollen Canal over the Dee valley 120 ft below. The final stage is over the Clywdian Hills, from which the mountains of Snowdonia dominate the view. The dyke itself has disappeared at this point, but the path ends agreeably by the sea.

Llanthony Abbey below Offa's Dyke

OXFORDSHIRE WAY

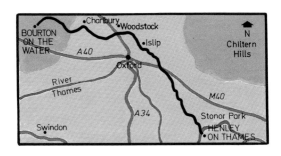

Length:	65 miles 105 kms
Status:	Regional route
From:	Bourton-on-the-Water
To:	Henley-on-Thames
Terrain:	Woods and fields, gently undulating
Maps:	OS Landranger 163, 164, 165, 175
Access:	BR Kingham via Oxford or Cheltenham. A40 Oxford-Cheltenham BR Henley via Slough. M4 junction 10 or M40 junction 4

Route Guides: *The Oxfordshire Way* by A.Kemp (Oxfordshire County Council)

Information: Oxfordshire County Council, County Hall, Oxford.

On opposite sides of Oxfordshire lie the two popular walking areas of the Cotswolds and the Chilterns. This trail links them by crossing the county along a route abounding in lovely villages. Bourton-on-the-Water, just over the border in Gloucestershire, is one of the prime Cotswold stone villages, standing on that great Roman road the Fosse Way. The River Windrush runs beside the main street, spanned by graceful little bridges. Leaving the river valley the trail climbs to

Wych Beacon at 800 ft the worst climb to be
encountered, though there are a few lesser hills on the
eight miles to Charlbury whose railway station is a
listed building. Fossil hunters will find a mecca at
Stonesfield where roof slates for Oxford colleges used
to be quarried. From here the line of Akeman Street,
another Roman road, provides the track as far as
Woodstock where a visit can be made to Blenheim
Palace. Sir Winston Churchill is buried nearby.
Characteristic Cotswold country is left behind here as
the trail crosses the River Cherwell to make a
detour north of Oxford and head into the Chiltern
Hills, following the edge of them along the
Buckinghamshire border through such quiet villages
as Islip, Otmoor, Rycote and Beckley, with many a
glimpse of Oxford's dreaming spires in the distance.
On the final stretch, just after Christmas Common, is
Stonor Park, one of the leading recusant houses which
still has priest holes to show. The final pleasure is to
descend to the Thames at Henley and relax by the
river.

Bourton-on-the-Water

PEDDARS WAY AND NORTH NORFOLK COAST PATH

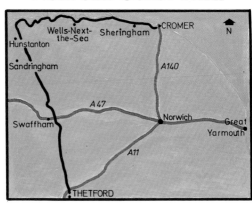

Length:	93 miles 150 kms
Status:	National Trail
From:	Knettishall Heath
To:	Cromer
Terrain:	Heath, fenland and sandy coast. Invariably flat
Maps:	OS Landranger 132, 133, 144
Access:	BR Harling Road, via Norwich. A11 London-Norwich BR Cromer. A140 from Norwich
Route Guides:	*Peddars Way & Norfolk Coast Path* by B.Robinson (HMSO) *Walking the Peddars Way and Norfolk Coastal Path* by D. Haiselden (Frederick Warne) *A Guide to the Norfolk Way* by D.H.Kennett (Constable) *Walking the Peddars Way and North Norfolk Coast Path with Weavers Way* (Peddars Way Association)
Information:	Peddars Way Association, 150 Armes St, Norwich NR2 4EG

Easy walking under the wide Norfolk skies, much of it by the breezy North Sea coast. The Peddars Way is an ancient track which may originally have linked up with the Ridgeway (q.v.). Then the Romans improved it as a fast highway for moving troops to keep down the natives. Many lengths remain untouched and are listed as ancient monuments. The national trail picks up the Peddars Way on Knettishall Heath, close by the Suffolk border and follows it across the sandy heathland called the Brecklands, avoiding most of the villages. Then it crosses an area of big farms, some of the richest arable country in England. Holkham Hall where Thomas Coke of Norfolk revolutionised farming in the 18th century is close by. The Peddars Way reaches the coast near Hunstanton, where the great bulge of Norfolk meets The Wash and it turns east towards Nelson's birthplace at Burnham Thorpe. Here the North Norfolk Coast Path takes over, though the two have always been lumped together as one national trail. Salt marshes and sand dunes make the character of this coast, famous for seabirds, crabs and legendary lifeboat heroes. The cliffs of Cromer mark the end, but Norfolk County Council have waymarked two regional routes, the Weavers' Way and the Angles Way (q.v.) to connect with the national trail and makes a complete Around Norfolk Walk (q.v.) So smooth and level is the Peddars Way that the Countryside Commission recommend parts of it for disabled or infirm people wanting an adventure trek.

On the Peddars Way   (Photo: Jarrold Publishing)

PEMBROKESHIRE COAST PATH

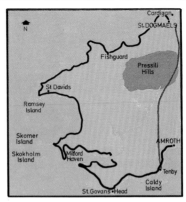

Length:	180 miles 290 kms
Status:	National trail
From:	Amroth
To:	St Dogmaels
Terrain:	Rugged cliff tops, some steep climbs
Maps:	OS Landranger 145, 157, 158
Access:	BR Tenby. A48 & A40 from end of M4 No rail link St Dogmaels. 28 miles by A478 to Tenby
Route Guides:	*Pembrokeshire Coast Path* by B.S.John (Aurum Press) *Guide to Pembrokeshire Coast Path* by C.J.Wright (Constable)
Information:	Information Officer, Pembrokeshire National Park, County Offices, Haverfordwest, Dyfed

The most dramatic coastal scenery in Wales lies round
its westernmost bulge in what was the old county of
Pembrokeshire. The whole coast, except for a gap
round Milford Haven, is a National Park and the coast
path traces its entire length. Starting at Amroth Castle
it takes an immediate climb up to a broken cliff line
before dropping again to the seaside resorts of

Saundersfoot and Tenby. Caldy Island just offshore is worth breaking off to visit. An easy stretch follows round Giltar Point and across the sands of Freshwater Bay before climbing again over St Govan's Head. There follows 18 miles of rather tough walking to Angle, then the path heads inland to skirt the waters of Milford Haven whose oil refineries are the only jarring note. Taking a bus to the other side avoids the worst. A mixture of woods, cliffs and mudflats takes the path to Dale. Offshore here are the well-known bird sanctuary islands of Skokholm and Skomer which can be visited. Cliffs, occasionally broken by sandy beaches, now stretch along St Brides Bay. St David's with its beautiful setting and cathedral is the main jewel of the walk. The area is rich in Celtic history and relics. St Non's Bay which follows has a tiny cliff-top chapel dedicated to the mother of St David. Distant views from 400 ft high cliffs mark the next section to Strumble Head from where the path drops into Fishguard. The Dinas Peninsula is the last big hurdle and an alternative route cuts across the neck of it to save a few miles.

Pembrokeshire Coast Path near Cardigan   (*Photo: Ramblers' Association*)

PENNINE WAY

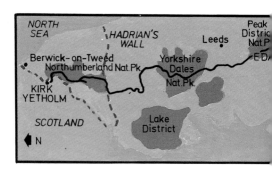

Length:	250 miles 402 kms
Status:	National trail
From:	Edale
To:	Kirk Yetholm
Terrain:	Moorlands, fells, mountains and limestone dales. Plenty of climbing and rough going
Maps:	OS Landranger 74, 80, 86, 87, 91, 92, 103, 109, 110, 119
Access:	BR Edale via Sheffield or Manchester. Off A625 BR Berwick-on-Tweed & 2 buses. B roads between Wooler/Kelso
Route Guides:	*Pennine Way* by B.Duerden (Ward Lock) *Pennine Way 2 vols* by T. Hopkins (Aurum Press) *Pennine Way Companion* by A.Wainright (Westmorland Gazette) *Guide to the Pennine Way* by J. C. Wright (Constable) *N. to S. Along the Pennine Way* by G.Hardy (Warne)
Information:	The Pennine Way Council, 89 Radford Rd, Lewisham, London SE13 6SB

One of the longest and one of the most challenging of

British national trails. It is also the mother of them all, being the idea of a man called Tom Stephenson back in 1935, though it took 30 years to realise. His aim was a walk along the rooftop of England, stretching right along the Pennine ridge from the Derbyshire Peak District, over the moors and dales of Yorkshire and across the fells of Northumberland to finish just over the Scottish border. It crosses a lot of remote hilly country and calls for experience, advance planning and sensible precautions, though it is very popular and thousands do it every year. Uncompromisingly it starts with a climb to the 2,088 ft plateau of Kinder Scout, followed by two equally hard slogging moors, Bleaklow and Black Hill. The next section crosses the Bronte country with its lowering gritstone edges. Next come the rounder, but still steep, limestone dales with some magnificent sights on the route. Malham Tarn is supposed to have inspired *The Water Babies*. Fantastic waterfalls like Hardrow Force and Cauldron Snout gush from the rocks. There is the summit of Penyghent 2,273 ft to be scaled and well earned refreshment to be taken on the top of Tan Hill 1,723 ft at England's highest and loneliest pub. Then the trail reaches Hadrian's Wall which it follows for a while. There is a respite from the hills through the Redesdale Forest before a last formidable push over the Cheviot Hills rising to 2,676 ft.

Near Keld in Swaledale on the Pennine Way   *(Photo: Alex Wilson)*

RIDGEWAY

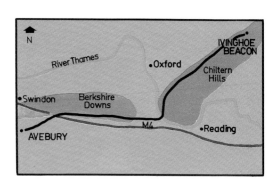

Length:	85 miles 137 kms
Status:	National trail
From:	Ivinghoe Beacon
To:	Avebury
Terrain:	Few climbs though on mainly high ground. Wide clear paths
Maps:	OS Landranger 165, 173, 174, 175
Access:	BR Tring. M1 junction 16 BR Swindon or Pewsey. M4, junction 15
Route Guides:	*The Ridgeway* by N. Curtis (Aurum Press) *Exploring The Ridgeway* by D. Charles (Countryside Books)
Information:	Ridgeway Officer, Library HQ, Holton, Oxford OX9 1QQ

Reputedly the oldest highway in Britain, used by primitive man over 4,000 years ago. Historians think it may have been part of a track all the way from East Anglia to Dorset. The national trail follows most of the parts that are identifiable, using alternative paths where not. It starts on the chalk downs above

Whipsnade Zoo and follows paths across the Chiltern
hills and through Buckinghamshire farms and
woodlands until it reaches the Thames valley at
Wallingford. Following the river meadows
downstream makes a contrasting change of scenery
before crossing the Thames at Goring and climbing up
to the Ridgeway proper on the Berkshire Downs. The
next 40 miles provide a grandstand view with wide
expanses on either hand, the spires of Oxford to the
north, the hills of Hampshire to the south. Well known
prehistoric monuments litter the way - Bronze Age
forts at Barbury Castle and Liddington Hill, the
neolithic tomb called Wayland's Smithy, the great
stone circle at Avebury, the strange white horse of
Uffington and Silbury Hill, biggest man made mound
in Europe whose purpose is still an enigma. For
archaeology enthusiasts the east-west crossing is
recommended as the interest reaches a natural climax
that way. Anyone who cares to keep on walking can
make a grand finale at Stonehenge. There are hardly
any villages on this western section, but a few roads
cross it, and plenty of paths lead down into the valley
for refreshment a mile or two away.

Prehistoric tracks along the Ridgeway   *(Photo: Ramblers' Association)*

ROBIN HOOD WAY

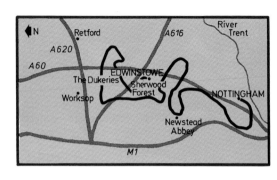

Length:	88 miles 141 kms
Status:	Regional route
From:	Nottingham Castle
To:	Sherwood Forest
Terrain:	Woods, canal paths, emparked land, low hills
Maps:	OS Landranger 129, 130
Access:	BR Nottingham. M1 junction 25 or 26 BR Worksop and bus. M1 junction 30
Route Guides:	*The Robin Hood Way* by C. J. Thompson (Notts County Council)
Information:	Nottinghamshire County Council, Trent Bridge House, Nottingham

Inevitably Nottinghamshire's first long distance footpath was devoted to its legendary outlaw. The number of clues to be found along the zig zag route through the county should be enough to dispel any scepticism about whether he and his merry men ever existed. The start is from the Robin Hood statue which stands by Nottingham Castle high above the city. Before heading out along the Beeston Canal, via University Park and Wollaton Hall, walkers should visit the *Trip To Jerusalem*, a unique inn carved out of

the solid rock beneath the castle. It has been serving
ale to departing wayfarers since men were going off to
the Crusades. A second canal leads the trail
northwards through the Erewash Valley to Bulwell
Hall Park and into the Blidworth Forest, beyond which
is Robin Hood's Stable. Newstead Abbey, home of
Lord Byron is the next stop. The path then enters
Fountain Dale which contains Friar Tuck's Well. Then
it reaches that distinctive part of Nottinghamshire
known as The Dukeries, because so many ducal
families created grand estates hareabouts. Most of
their parklands are accessible to-day for public
recreation. Two through which the trail passes are
Rufford Abbey and Clumber Park, both a wonderful
sight in autumn foliage. Finally the trail enters
Sherwood Forest itself. At the centre is the Major Oak,
a massive, hollow tree centuries old. The finishing
point is the village of Edwinstowe in whose church, so
the tale goes, Robin Hood and Maid Marion were wed.

The Major Oak in Sherwood Forest

SAINTS WAY

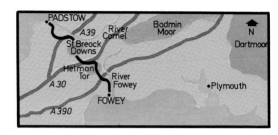

Length:	37 miles 59 kms
Status:	Unofficial
From:	Padstow
To:	Fowey
Terrain:	A few steep climbs, but mainly easy
Maps:	OS Landranger 200, 201
Access:	BR Bodmin Parkway and bus. Off A39 coast road BR Par and bus. Off A390
Route Guides:	*The Saints Way* by M.Gill (Co-operative Retail Society)
Information:	CRS Member Relations Dept, 105, Station Rd, St Blazey, Par, Cornwall PL24 2LZ

The Saints Way, or to give it its Cornish name Forth An Syns, is a good way of seeing an undiscovered Cornwall away from the tripper filled seaside haunts. It was pioneered in 1986 under a Co-op community programme and is said to follow a prehistoric trading route used by early merchants who wanted to avoid rounding Land's End in their flimsy craft. Later along came missionaries spreading the Christian message from Ireland. They used the same route on their way through the country, converting the Cornish, setting up monastic communities, building churches and erecting granite crosses by the wayside. The trail begins at Padstow where saint and sinner alike must have been thankful to set foot on dry land. This beautiful fishing port sits beside the broad, sandy estuary of the River Camel with its ominous Doom Bar. The steep climb to the summit of Dennis Hill at the start of the walk enables you to look back and appreciate the setting. To the south-east the line of the St Breock Downs with the church of St Issey nestling below is a target to aim for, some half dozen miles ahead. This is the highest point of the walk 700 ft above sea level and marked by a 16 ft megalith. After a lowland stretch there is another climb to Helman Tor from which the rest of the way down the valley of the River Fowey is seen spread out. On its final leg the path climbs the hill above Fowey town only to plunge down again through its steep, twisted streets to the edge of the beautiful estuary.

Megalith on St Breock Down

SANDSTONE TRAIL

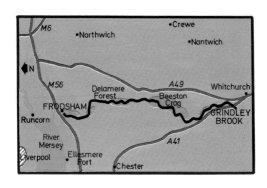

Length:	30 miles 48 kms
Status:	Regional route
From:	Frodsham
To:	Grindley Brook
Terrain:	Rocky hill ridges, fairly steep, between lower stretches
Maps:	OS Landranger 117
Access:	BR Delamere via Chester and bus. M56 junction 12 BR Whitchurch via Crewe and bus. Off A41
Route Guides:	*Sandstone Trail Walker's Guide* (Cheshire County Council)
Information:	Director of Countryside & Recreation, Goldsmith House, Hamilton Place, Chester CH1 1SE

Driving through Cheshire leaves the impression of a plain broken only by the giant dishes of Jodrell Bank radio telescope. Walkers' Cheshire holds far more variety. This trail bisects the county, following a ridge of sandstone created in some geological upheaval aeons ago. This backbone makes a fine ridge walk and a continuous viewing platform for the surrounding countryside. There are plenty of places en route, when the path descends to lower levels, to sample the quintessential Cheshire of prolific hedgerows, black and white timbered houses, big dairy farms, meres and patches of wetland known locally as 'mosses'. The starting point is on Beacon Hill outside Frodsham. A steep descent into Dunsdale Hollow gives the geologically minded a chance to make a closer study of the weathered sandstone. A day's tramp brings the trail to Delamere Forest, like so many similar places the remains of a royal hunting ground. It then follows for a while the line of the Roman Watling Street to the Shropshire Union, one of the many canals which cross Cheshire. Towering ahead is Beeston Crag, 300 ft high and topped by a ruined castle built to keep the Welsh at bay. The view from the top is rated the loveliest in the county. Silver birch, heather, bracken and, at the right time, bilberries cover the Burwardsley and Peckforton Hills, the next two heights ahead. Where the trail ends at Grindley Brook the footpath, main road, railway and canal all meet. The canal has a grand staircase of locks.

Delamere Forest, Cheshire   *(Photo: Jarrold Publishing)*

SAXON SHORE WAY

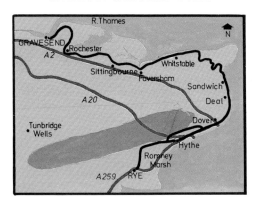

Length:	143 miles 230 kms
Status:	Regional route
From:	Gravesend
To:	Rye
Terrain:	Marsh creeks and seawalls, then downs and chalk cliffs
Maps:	OS Landranger 178, 179, 189
Access:	BR Gravesend. A2 out of London BR Rye. A259 Hastings-Folkestone road
Route Guides:	*Saxon Shore Way* set of cards (Ramblers' Association)
Information:	Tourism Section, Kent County Council, Springfield, Maidstone, Kent ME14 2LL

This trail hugs the coastline of Kent from the point where the River Medway joins the Thames to Rye over the Sussex border. The Roman commander here had the title Count of the Saxon Shore which lives on in the name of the trail, but there are forts, castles and monuments of every period along the way. Marshy creeks dominate the early landscape, with interesting stops in Medway towns like Chatham with its long

naval history and dockyard museum. There are strong
Dickens links around here too. Following the deep
inlet of the Swale through Sittingbourne and
Favershsam brings the trail to the open sea at
Whitstable, famous for its oysters, but the path cuts off
the peninsula formed by the Isle of Thanet to avoid the
more urbanised resorts of Margate and Ramsgate. The
coast is picked up again at Sandwich, one of the
historic Cinque Ports. Out to sea as the path goes
through Deal you may see the notorious Goodwin
Sands, graveyard of many ships. Ahead are the white
cliffs of Dover. The town has a substantial castle and
the remains of a Roman lighthouse. Beyond Dover
walkers have a choice of following the coast along to
Hythe or sampling a stretch of the South Downs on an
inland loop. The final section is along the edge of the
Romney Marshes, following the Royal Military Canal
built for defensive purposes during Napoleonic
invasion scares. There is a final climb into Rye high
on a hill above the flood plains of the Rother estuary.
In medieval times it was an important port, but long
ago the sea receded and left it high and dry.

White cliffs on the Saxon Shore   *(Photo: Kent County Council)*

SEVERN WAY

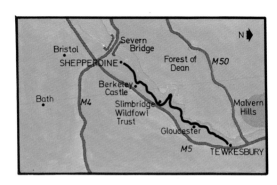

Length:	50 miles 80 kms
Status:	Regional route
From:	Tewkesbury
To:	Shepperdine
Terrain:	Meadowland and riverside paths. Flat but sometimes slippery or flooded
Maps:	OS Landranger 150, 162
Access:	BR Gloucester and bus. M5 junction 9 No convenient rail link. M5 junction 14
Route Guides:	*Severn Way* by S.H. Gidman (Gloucester County Libraries)
Information:	Environmental Services, Shire Hall, Gloucester GL1 2TH

The Severn is Britain's longest river, but alas has no source-to-sea trail. This Severn Way makes a start with a 50 mile route along the eastern bank of the middle reaches of the river in Gloucestershire. One attraction is the chance to see the Severn Bore, a tidal wave, sometimes nine feet high, which rushes up the river at certain states of the tide. A run of them occurs at roughly fortnightly intervals and it is worth inquiring in advance about good dates to see this rare phenomenon. The walk starts outside Tewkesbury

Abbey, built in 1471 and still the parish church, picking up the riverside meadows and heading south for Derehurst. Gloucester itself is on the route, the cathedral requiring a short diversion. The path goes through the old docks which flourished when the Severn was an important mercantile highway. Then the river had its own distinctive sailing craft called Severn trows. One is used as the waymark symbol of the walk. Returning to rural pastures it passes the ruins of Llanthony Priory on the way to Stonebench, which is one of the best viewing places for the bore. Other attractions on this trail are the Slimbridge Wildfowl Sanctuary founded by Sir Peter Scott and Berkeley Castle, scene of many bloody escapades. By this point the river is broadening into an estuary and the track runs along wild and lonely floodbanks and sea walls to end at the *Windrush Inn* where sailing ship crews used to wait for a favourable wind. There are plans to establish another trail along the western bank.

Slimbridge, excuse for a break on the Severn Way

SHEFFIELD WAY

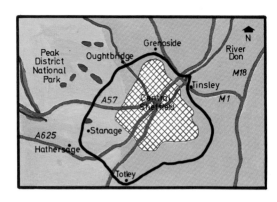

Length:	45 miles 72 kms
Status:	Regional route
From:	Sheffield
To:	Sheffield (circular)
Terrain:	Hill tracks and moorland, with lower lying woods & fields
Maps:	OS Landranger 110, 111, 119, 120
Access:	BR Sheffield Central. M1 junction 34 Good bus services to intermediate points
Route Guides:	*The Sheffield Way* by P.Price (Sheffield City Libraries)
Information:	Public Right of Way Unit, PO Box 241, Sheffield S1 1SB

The idea of a trail round a major industrial city may seem uninviting, but the Victorian aesthete John Ruskin called Sheffield a dirty picture in a golden frame and the late Poet Laureate Sir John Betjeman enthused about its suburbs. Other cities have walkers' trails, (London, Birmingham, Hull, Leeds among them), but all at some distance from the perimeter. The Sheffield Way is unusual in staying inside the administrative boundary for 90 percent of its length, yet being a remarkably rural walk. There can't be

many municipalities within whose limits you might
need to find your way off a moor by compass if the
weather closes in. Of course the Peak District National
Park is bang on the doorstep. In fact 6,000 acres of it
is within the city. Anyone hesitating to devote time to
45 miles so close to a highly populated industrial area
would be advised to opt for the western half of the
circle, walking from Grenoside to Totley. The guide,
an A4 size publication with six inch to the mile maps,
gives the walk a starting point only 200 yards from the
M1 at Tinsley. Following the canal and the River Don
it threads through wooded, steep sided valleys to
Oughtibridge before cutting westwards over moorland
tops and through hill farms to Dam Flask. Grouse
moors, now happily easier of access than they used to
be, lie ahead, the highlight being the crossing of
Stanage Moor by a Roman road to the great gritstone
face of Stanage Edge from where the hills of
neighbouring Derbyshire unfold.

Burbage Moor on the Sheffield Way

SHROPSHIRE WAY

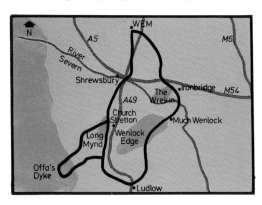

Length:	125 miles 200 kms
Status:	Unofficial
From:	Wem
To:	Wem (circular route)
Terrain:	Low farmland broken by upland areas of rocky moor
Maps:	OS Landranger 117, 126, 137, 138
Access:	BR Wem. Off A49 Shrewsbury-Whitchurch road

Route Guides: *The Shropshire Way* by R.Kirk (Thornhill Press)

Information: No central source

Though this is planned as a circular route it could be logical to do one half and stop at Ludlow which has a convenient BR station. Conversely there are a few extension loops which increase the total to 172 miles and links with the Sandstone Trail (q.v.) and Offa's Dyke Path (q.v.). Shropshire is a county of scenic surprises. Farmland plains suddenly erupt into massive heather covered hills whose rocky edges face across the Welsh Border Marches. These make for some exhilarating ridge walks and a contrast to the fields and half timbered villages of the lowland stretches.

This is the land of Houseman's melancholy *Shropshire Lad* and of Brother Cadfael, the medieval monk and amateur sleuth created by Ellis Peters. Cadfael's original Benedictine house, Shrewsbury Abbey, still functions as the parish church of the historic county town and is on the route, 15 miles from the suggested starting point. Another day's tramp takes in the Long Mynd, one of the best of the upland sections. Ludlow at the southern point has almost untouched Tudour streets and a story book castle. A bonus on the return route, after crossing Wenlock Edge, is Ironbridge, often called the birthplace of the Industrial Revolution and the route crosses the world's first iron bridge, built by Abraham Darby over the River Severn. This is the centre of a complex of working open air museums realistically recreating the life of the times and they could hold up walking for at least a day.

Clun, nestling in Shropshire hills   *(Photo: Ramblers' Association)*

SOLENT WAY

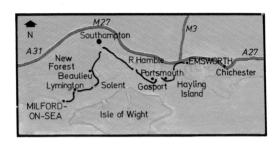

Length:	55 miles 88 kms
Status:	Regional route
From:	Milford-on-Sea
To:	Emsworth
Terrain:	Flat coastline, woods and field paths. Easy going
Maps:	OS Landranger 196, 197
Access:	BR New Milton. From M27 junction 1 BR Emsworth. A27 coast road
Route Guides:	*The Solent Way* by B.Shurlock (Hampshire County Council)
Information:	Hants County Council Recreation Dept., North Hill Close, Andover Rd, Winchester SO22 6AQ

An easy going walk along the extent of Hampshire's coast with views across the Solent to the Isle of Wight. The first objective is Hurst Castle on Hurst Point. This involves a determined crunch along a shingle beach, but a little ferry to Keyhaven saves having to go back again. From here the route passes through Lymington to Buckler's Hard, a well conserved hamlet on the banks of the lovely Beaulieu River where sailing men o'war were once built. Beaulieu Abbey further upstream is a stately home with tourist attractions. Paths through the New Forest emerge on the banks of Southampton Water at Hythe, where a ferry crossing avoids tedious roads. Southampton has all the big city amenities, but retains its old walls and other antiquities. Passing along the waterfront to the Royal Victoria Country Park brings you out on the yacht-crowded River Hamble which can be crossed by ferry to Warsash. A quiet stretch to Lee-on-Solent and the nature reserve at Titchfield Haven ends at Gosport where a tour round the submarine HMS *Alliance* makes a break. A ferry crosses the harbour to the Royal Dockyard at Portsmouth where there are Henry VIII's flagship *Mary Rose*, Nelson's *Victory* and the first ironclad HMS *Warrior*. Half a mile further on Southsea Castle houses the D Day Museum. Turning north at Eastney the path follows the shores of Langstone Harbour where the low tide mudflats are a haven for wading birds. Beyond are the many creeks and inlets of Chichester Harbour where the trail ends.

Beaulieu River in the New Forest

SOMERSET AND NORTH DEVON COAST PATH

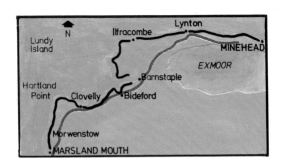

Length:	82 miles 132 kms
Status:	National trail
From:	Minehead
To:	Marsland Mouth
Terrain:	Dramatic clifftop walking, some of it fairly rugged going
Maps:	OS Landranger 180, 181, 190
Access:	BR Taunton then bus. M5 junction 23 BR Barnstaple then bus. Off A39 for Morwenstow
Route Guides:	*South West Way vol 1* by M.Collins (Cicerone Press) *South West Way vol 1* by R.Tarr (Aurum Press)
Information:	South West Way Association, 1 Orchard Drive, Kingskerswell, Newton Abbot, Devon TQ12 5DG West Country Tourist Board, Trinity Court, Southerhay East, Exeter EX1 1QS

First (or possibly last) section of the South West Peninsula Coast Path (q.v.), but in either direction it makes an excellent trail on its own. As you start from Minehead the view is over the Bristol Channel to the hills of Wales. The open Atlantic pounding the surf up the beaches comes later. Exmoor and Lorna Doone country keeps company on the landward side. After Porlock Weir comes a scramble through the Valley of the Rocks heading towards the first prominent headland at Foreland Point. On the way the path switchbacks over Countisbury Hill where lifeboat history was made with the "overland launch". After this come Lynton and Lynmouth clinging to the steep sides of a gorge. The going is flatter beside the wide bays of Croyde and Woolacombe. At Ilfracombe a boat trip to Lundy Island makes a break. From Braunton a bus will avoid some tedious road work to reach the other side of the Taw Estuary where Bideford and Appledore are historic ports to explore. In a dozen miles is Clovelly, touristy picture postcard village, but when approached on foot still delightful. Part of the path to it is along the Hobby Drive, made by an 18th century squire to open up the best vistas. Hartland Point ahead is one of the most dramatic headlands on the route and tiny Hartland Quay tucked behind it records a long history of wreck and rescue in its museum. The wide open expanses of clifftop on the last leg provide exhilarating and at times quite arduous walking, along with some of the most spectacular coastal scenery anywhere.

Porlock Weir on the coast path in Somerset

SOUTH DEVON COAST PATH

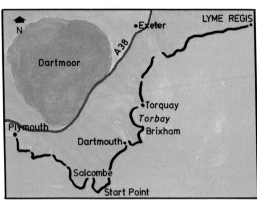

Length:	93 miles 150kms
Status:	National trail
From:	Plymouth
To:	Lyme Regis
Terrain:	Mainly clifftops with some fairly rough ups and downs
Maps:	OS Landranger 192, 193, 201, 202
Access:	BR Plymouth. A38 (continuation of M5) BR Axmouth then bus. Off A35
Route Guides:	*South West Way vol 2* by M.Collins (Cicerone Press) *South West Way vols 2 & 3* (Aurum Press)
Information:	South West Way Association, 1 Orchard Drive, Kingkerswell, Newton Abbot, Devon TQ12 5DG West Country Tourist Board, Trinity Court, Southernhay East, Exeter EX1 1QS

One of the four sections making up the South West Way but long enough to make a good venture of its own. Though it passes close to more populated areas than the other sections it nevertheless has wild, unfrequented stretches and some outstanding scenery. There are no less than ten estuaries to be crossed by bridge, ferry or in two cases fording. Turnchapel, the westward terminal, is tucked in a corner of Plymouth Sound opposite the famous Hoe and a bus is advisable. Passing lots of old fortifications with views of the Sound and distant Cornwall you come to Wembury and the first river crossing, over the Yealm by ferry. From here a former carriage drive created by a Victorian banker makes a broad cliff-top path towards the rivers Erme and Avon which can be crossed on foot at low tide. Then come the gaunt granite outlines of Bolt Tail and Bolt Head standing between Hope Cove and bewitching Salcombe. From there another ferry trip is needed to pick up the path again for Dartmouth where there is also plenty to see before yet another ferry. Then you are heading for Berry Head and Brixham's trawler port. The bit of urbanised seaside round Torquay will justify a bus ride from Goodrington to the resumption of the path at Hope's Nose, from where there are steep undulations as far as the next ferry crossing over the River Teign. Then beyond the River Exe (ferry from Starcross to Exmouth) you are among the rich red clay farmlands of East Devon and stately watering places like Budleigh Salterton and Sidmouth.

South Devon Coast Path near Noss Mayo

SOUTH DOWNS WAY

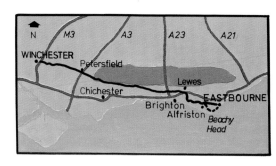

Length:	99 miles 158 kms
Status:	National trail
From:	Winchester
To:	Eastbourne
Terrain:	Gentle hills over chalk downs, smooth and dry underfoot
Maps:	OS Landranger 185, 197, 198, 199
Access:	BR Winchester. M3 juntion 9 BR Eastbourne. Off A27 south coast road
Route Guides:	*South Downs Way & Downs Link* by K.Reynolds (Cicerone Press) *South Downs Way* by P. Millmore (Aurum Press) *Guide to the South Downs Way* by M.Jebb (Constable)
Information:	South East England Tourist Board, 1 Warwick Park, Tunbridge Wells TN1 1NH Southern Tourist Board, 40 Chamberlayne Rd, Eastleigh, Hants SO5 5JH

The South Downs are the rounded, short cropped grass uplands that lie behind the chalk cliffs of the Channel coast. Paths are wide and unmistakable (because the trail is also a bridleway) and the chalk makes for a dry surface. Guide books make this trail east to west, but there is much to be said for the other direction. This way there is a magnificent climax after you descend from the downs and follow the swooping Sussex clifftops by Birling Gap, Seven Sisters and Beachy Head. Another reason is that the Hampshire section (a recent extension of the trail) is more wooded and enclosed while the eastern end is over true open downland. Although the walker is never far from attractive villages and civilised amenities there is a great sense of spaciousness up there and panoramic views. The rivers Arun, Adur and Cuckmere make spectacular sights from above as they meander in huge ox bow patterns to the sea. This part of England has been settled for over 4,000 years and the trail is rich in ancient monuments like Butser Hill, Ditchling Beacon and Chanctonbury Rings (prehistoric camps), the mysterious Long Man of Wilmington chalk figure, Roman villas, windmills and old churches. In contrast to Winchester Cathedral at the start the trail passes tiny Lullington church, just 16 ft square, and Alfriston parish church, 'the cathedral of the downs'. Glyndebourne is also on the way for anyone wanting an operatic interlude. A link path connects with the North Downs Way (q.v.).

Preparing to walk the South Downs   *(Photo: Ian Howard)*

SOUTH WEST PENINSULA COAST PATH

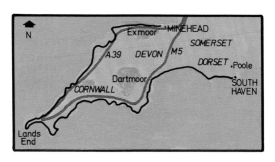

Length:	560 miles 896 kms
Status:	National trail
From:	Minehead
To:	Poole Harbour
Terrain:	Varied, with preponderance of cliff paths, some arduous
Maps:	See individual section details
Access:	BR Taunton then bus. M5 junction 23 BR Bournemouth or Poole then bus & ferry. Bournemouth and car ferry or A351 via Wareham
Route Guides:	*South West Way 2 vols* by M.Collins (Cicerone Press) *South West Way 4 vols* by various authors (Aurum Press)
Information:	South West Way Association, 1 Orchard Drive, Kingskerswell, Newton Abbot, Devon TQ12 5DG West Country Tourist Board, Trinity Court, Southernhay East, Exeter EX1 1QS

Longest of all the British national trails created by the Countryside Commission and now usually just called the South West Way for short. It was first envisaged in a government report in 1945 but only completed as a continuous right of way in 1978, running through four counties and linking up the miles of coast and cliff-top tracks created after HM Customs & Excise recruited Riding Officers to patrol the coast when smuggling was at its peak in the 18th and 19th centuries. It takes a practised walker five weeks to complete the whole in one expedition and most people tackle it piecemeal. The South West Way is formed of four distinctive sections - the Somerset & North Devon Coast Path, the Cornwall Coast Path, the South Devon Coast Path and the Dorset Coast Path. Each of these is treated separately in this book and should be referred to for fuller information. They are all long enough to make a holiday on their own, or a series of week-ends. The South West Way Association is an active body publishing information about transport, accommodation and matters of general interest about the path as well as acting as a watchdog. Nearly all of this is what might be termed Heritage Coast whether officially guarded by the National Trust (as much of it is) or not. If you are attempting the whole the experts counsel starting at Minehead on the grounds that you then have the prevailing south-westerlies at your back for the longest part of the journey, after turning the corner at Lands End.

Devon cliffs near Bigbury

SOUTHERN UPLAND WAY

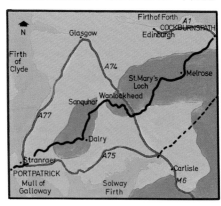

Length:	212 miles 341 kms
Status:	National Trail
From:	Portpatrick
To:	Cockburnspath
Terrain:	Mainly high hills, some remote with many climbs
Maps:	OS Landranger 61, 73, 74, 77, 78, 82
Access:	BR Stranraer then bus. A74 off M6 or A77 from Glasgow BR Dunbar and bus. Off A1 Edinburgh-Berwick
Route Guides:	*Southern Upland Way 2* vols by K.Andrew (HMSO) *Guide to Southern Upland Way* by D.Williams (Constable)
Information:	Scottish Countryside Commission, Battleby, Redgorton, Perth PH1 3EW

The longest of Scotland's national trails, crossing the Lowlands from coast to coast. Lowlands is a comparative word, for this is hillscape commonly running to 1,500 ft. It passes through large tracts of unspoilt country, well away from popular tourist areas and little explored by Sassenach walkers. To tackle the whole is no mean achievement. There are many miles of successive hills to be scaled because the route is at right angles to the north-south line of the hill ranges, but there are also compensating days of river valleys and softer country. The central section is very unpopulated and needs advance planning. There are two stages where no shops, cafes or other amenities will be found for 30 miles. Starting from Portpatrick in the west makes sense, so that the prevailing weather is at your back. First the route heads north-east over the Galloway Hills and through the Glen Trool Forest Park to Dalry and the range of hills known as the Rhinns of Kells, reaching its halfway point at Beattock, near Moffat, the latter once a spa and important wool town. The second half climbs over 2,000 ft to St Mary's Loch, then crosses the Attrick Forest (more hills than trees) to Lauder. The last big range between here and the east coast fishing villages is the Lammermuir Hills. The Southern Uplands suffered greatly during the Covenant troubles and has many martyrs' memorials. It is also the homeland of Robert Burns and the locale of Richard Hannay's adventures in the John Buchan novels.

Glen Trool on the Southern Uplands   *(Photo: John Pugh)*

SPEYSIDE WAY

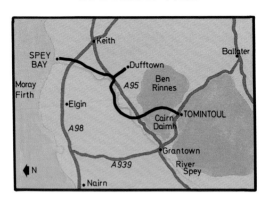

Length:	45 miles 72 kms
Status:	National trail
From:	Spey Bay
To:	Tomintoul
Terrain:	Easy riverside paths followed by moor and mountain tracks
Maps:	OS Landranger 28, 36
Access:	BR Elgin and bus. Off A96 east of Elgin BR Keith and bus. A939 Grantown-Ballater road
Route Guides:	*Speyside Way* leaflet (Moray District Council)
Information:	Ranger Service, Boat o'Fiddich, Craigellachie, Banffshire

One of Scotland's all too few national trails and not yet complete. It follows the valley of a famous salmon river. There are three distilleries open to the public on the route and another ten close by. Another virtue of the Speyside Way is that it is a gentler introduction to the grandeur of Scottish scenery for walkers than either the West Highland or Southern Upland Ways. Working upstream and coming to the hills by easy stages seems to be the accepted direction. It starts at Tugnet where the river spills into Spey Bay on the Moray Firth. Waders and seabirds are profuse. Following the east bank to Fochabers the trail then climbs to Ordiequish where the valley can be viewed in panorama before dropping to Boat o' Fiddich and skirting the afforested slopes of Ben Aigen, 1,500 ft. On the other side at Craigelachie the tributary River Fiddich is crossed. The main cluster of distilleries is around here. The path continues along an old railway line which gives some of the best views in Speyside and is rich in wildlife. Four miles on and an impressive viaduct, now a listed building, carries the trail over the Spey and into Ballindalloch. One day it will branch off here over the Grampians to Glenmore. Meanwhile there is a 15 mile section to Tomintoul which provides a complete contrast. It goes by mountain tracks and old drove roads to the magnificent summit of Cairn Daimh, 1,850 ft above sea level. It is rough in places and the last section over an expanse of peat bog calls for care in bad weather.

Speyside in winter   *(Photo: John Pugh)*

STAFFORDSHIRE WAY

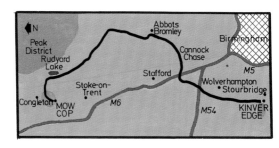

Length:	92 miles 153 kms
Status:	Regional route
From:	Mow Cop Castle
To:	Kinver
Terrain:	Sandstone edges with steep climbs, woods, heaths, farm paths
Maps:	O.S. Landranger 118, 127, 128, 138
Access:	BR Kidsgrove. M6 junction 17 BR Stourbridge and bus. M5 junction 4
Route Guides:	*Staffordshire Way Long Distance Footpath* (Staffs County Council).
Information:	Staffordshire County Council, Martin St, Stafford.

A county traverse of surprises for anyone whose vision of Staffordshire is limited to the Potteries. In the north the trail starts at Mow Cop, a rocky gritstone eminence on Congleton Edge crowned by a 'ruined castle' folly. Westwards the views along the edge are over the wide plain of neighbouring Cheshire and eastwards to the slopes of the Peak District. Descending from the heights the path flanks Rudyard Lake and enters wooded country, joining the towpath of the restored Caldon Canal which leads to the secluded Churnet

Valley. There is more climbing to hilltops looking out over an area nicknamed the Staffordshire Rhineland. From here the way drops down into Denstone to meet the River Churnet again and follow it through pasture land to Rocester where it meets the River Dove. The Dove keeps company as far as the market town of Uttoxeter. Then the path crosses undulating farmland to Abbots Bromley, noted for its ancient folk ritual, the Horn Dance. Then there is a descent into the valley of the River Trent, which made Burton-on-Trent famous for its beer. This leads to Shugborough Hall, a stately home and grounds worth seeing before crossing Cannock Chase, an Area of Outstanding Natural Beauty covered in heath and woodlands. After leaving the Chase the way enters a region that has been dubbed the Staffordshire Parklands because of the large number of grand houses set in landscaped grounds. Another climb to a lofty sandstone edge brings the trail to an end near the village of Kinver.

'Ruined castle' folly on Mow Cop

STOUR VALLEY WALK

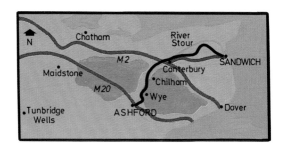

Length:	38 miles 60 kms
Status:	Regional route
From:	Ashford
To:	Sandwich
Terrain:	Open downs, woods, farmland & river banks. Moderate hills
Maps:	OS Landranger 179, 189
Access:	BR Ashford. M20 junction 10 BR Sandwich. A257 from A2 at Canterbury
Route Guides:	*Stour Valley Walk* (Kent County Council)
Information:	Kent County Council Planning Dept, Springfield, Maidstone ME8 0LW

A heron is the waymark symbol of this walk through a delectable part of Kent, there being several colonies of this striking bird along the route. The trail crosses varied scenery, including the traditional Kent landscape of orchards, oast houses and hop gardens. There are many places of historic interest along the way as well. Ashford where it starts is destined to become to become the first rail stop after France when the Channel Tunnel is complete. Leaving the town and crossing the noisy M20 the trail climbs up the escarpment of the North Downs through which the River Stour cuts its way to flow past a Domesday water mill and the historic little town of Wye. Signs of the old strip cultivation can still be spotted in the fields around here. Continuing towards Chilham the path follows an old carriage way along which Jane Austen once rode. The village has a fine Jacobean mansion, a restored mill and a good birdwatching lake. Chartham church has some notable brasses and the village green some keen cricketers. Canterbury is about the half-way stage and time will be needed to see its sights. Beyond the cathedral town the landscape begins to grow more level, in places marshy and fen-like, due to the fact that in Saxon times the coastline was much nearer. On what was then the shore stands Richborough Castle where the Romans came ashore in 43AD. Sandwich at the end of the trail looks deserted by the sea too but for centuries was an important port which still has its quays and medieval gates.

Abbey ruins and cathedral, Canterbury   *(Photo: Kent County Council)*

SWAN'S WAY

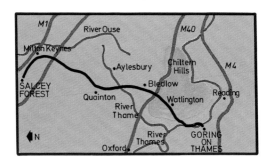

Length:	65 miles 105 kms
Status:	Regional route
From:	Salcey Forest
To:	Goring-on-Thames
Terrain:	Easily undulating hills, woods, farm and riverside
Maps:	OS Landranger 153, 166, 176
Access:	BR Milton Keynes & bus. M1 junction 14 BR Goring. Off A340 Oxford-Reading
Route Guides:	*Swan's Way* leaflet (Buckinghamshire County Council)
Information:	Planning Dept, County Hall, Aylesbury HP32 1UY

Devised as a long distance bridleway across Buckinghamshire this makes an equally good trail for bipeds. It begins in a 1,200 acre park, the remains of a royal hunting ground. Crossing the valley of the River Ouse at Haversham it passes through the tree lined outskirts of Milton Keynes, following the Grand Union canal and a disused railway branch line, past a restored windmill to Whaddon where Spenser wrote *The Faerie Queen*. At Whaddesdon, after some ups and downs, the way heads south into the fertile Vale of Aylesbury. On the way Quainton has a moated manor, a steam railway centre and a deserted medieval settlement. Reaching the River Thame marks the beginning of the Chiltern Hills. Bledlow is an attractive village passed through on the eastern escarpment. Above it Bledlow Cop with a round barrow on top rises to 799 ft. Now for some distance the Swan's Way follows the Ridgeway (q.v.) over Swyncombe Downs to Beacon Hill, 784 ft, and on to the Aston Rowant nature reserve. On the next eminence, Watlington Hill, a white mark cut in the chalk hillside guides walkers the right way and has a curious story attached. Next comes Ewelme, a picture postcard village noted for almshouses connected with Chaucer, watercress and honey. Outside it the path crosses Grim's Ditch, the mysterious earthwork which can be traced through several counties. The way finally descends gently to meet the River Thames on the Oxfordshire bank at South Stoke and follows it downstream to Goring.

Curious landmark at Watlington

TEST WAY AND CLARENDON WAY

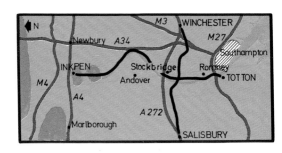

Length:	46 miles 73 kms
Status:	Regional route
From:	Totton
To:	Inkpen Beacon
Terrain:	Water meadows, some old railway track, chalk hills
Maps:	OS Landranger 174, 185, 196
Access:	BR Southampton and bus. M27 junction 2 BR Kintbury via Reading. M4 junction 13
Route Guides:	*The Test Way & Clarendon Way* by B.Shurlock (Hampshire County Council)
Information:	Hampshire County Council Recreation Department, North Hill Close, Andover Rd, Winchester SO22 6AQ

Two distinct trails which cross each other at right angles. Hampshire County Council promote them together to provide walkers with a permutation of six possible routes. Main details given above are for the longer Test Way. Facts different for the Clarendon Way are given below. The Test Way follows roughly

the valley of the River Test, reputedly the finest chalk
trout stream in England. Certainly its clear waters and
reed-fringed meadows are a delight. Some of the Way
also follows the defunct railway between Andover and
Romsey, once fondly known as the Sprat and Winkle
Line. That itself was built on the bed of a canal built in
1794, so as a route it has some history. Like the
Wayfarer's Walk (q.v.) it crosses Hampshire from end
to end and shares the same northern terminal on top of
Inkpen Beacon, the highest chalk hill in Britain. The
start at Totton is on the marshes and nature reserve at
the head of Southampton Water. At Romsey is
Broadlands the home of Earl Mountbatten, which is
open to the public. The Clarendon Way bisects the
Test Way near Kings Sombourne, half-way along its
26 mile (38 kms) route which links the cathedral cities
of Salisbury and Winchester. Both have BR stations
and are on major roads. The trail takes its name from
Clarendon Palace, a shooting lodge for Norman kings,
vestiges of which can be seen. The terrain is moderate
with a few slopes. A fitting conclusion is to ask for the
free Wayfarer's Dole of bread and beer at the Hospital
of St Cross in Winchester. Nobody has been refused
for 500 years.

River Test near Stockbridge

THAMES PATH

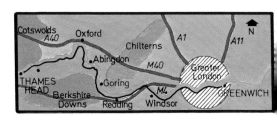

Length:	195 miles 314 kms
Status:	National trail designate
From:	London
To:	Thames Head (the source)
Terrain:	Meadows and towpaths, some woods and country lanes. Level
Maps:	OS Landranger 163, 164, 174, 175, 176
Access:	BR Charlton from Charing Cross. On A206 BR Kemble via Swindon. A419 from M4 junction 15
Route Guides:	*The Thames Path* by D.Sharp (Ramblers' Association)
Information:	Ramblers' Association, 1, Wandsworth Rd, London SW8 2XX

Following Old Father Thames is an inviting prospect but it has taken 40 years to get within sight of a completed national trail. As the river was for centuries used for commerce there was a tow path most of the way. After river traffic declined a lot of it was lost to public access. For many years the Ramblers' Association has been working at creating a trail, making use of existing rights of way and negotiating permitted access where necessary. This groundwork is now being used as the basis for the national trail. It begins at the Thames Barrier, just downstream from Greenwich. The advantage of walking from London rather than from the source is that every step upstream leads into more peaceful surroundings, ending idyllically in the meadows of Trewsbury Mead. Don't be too disappointed at the source of one of the world's most famous rivers. At best it is a trickle and most of the time just a damp patch. Somebody called the Thames 'liquid history' and there is certainly much to allow time for - royal palaces like Windsor, stately homes like Syon Park and Cliveden, famous towns like Oxford, Abingdon, Henley and Marlow and dozens of riverside pubs and villages. On the river itself there is always plenty of wildlife and, below Lechlade, nautical activity for diversion. If you don't fancy the noise and hard pavements of central London you can always begin at Putney or Teddington. The reverse route is theoretically downhill, but not so much as you would notice the difference walking.

The Thames at Lechlade

THREE SHIRES WAY

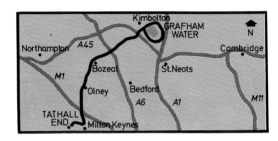

Length:	37 miles 59 kms
Status:	Regional route
From:	Tathall End
To:	Graffham Water
Terrain:	Farm and woodland tracks, gently undulating, firm
Maps:	OS Landranger 152, 153
Access:	BR Milton Keynes. M1 junction 14 BR St Neots or Huntingdon. A45 St Neots-Northampton road
Route Guides:	*Three Shires Way* leaflet (Beds, Bucks & Cambs County Councils)
Information:	Bedfordshire County Council, County Hall, Bedford MK42 9AP Bucks County Council, County Hall, Aylesbury HP320 1UY Cambridgeshire County Council, Shire Hall, Cambridge CB3 0AP

Primarily planned as a bridleway, though equally pleasurable for walkers, the occasional horse being inoffensive company. It goes through the counties of Buckinghamshire, Bedfordshire and Cambridgeshire, hence the name. The route uses several ancient trackways, passes many small, historic villages and meanders through some beautiful landscape. At the western (Buckinghamshire) end it connects with the Swan's Way (q.v.), another bridleway which ends at the River Thames at Goring. Together they would make a 100 mile trek. Travelling eastwards the Three Shires leaves Tathall End where the 190 ft high church spire is the highest in the county. Another early landmark is Gayhurst House whose builder, Sir Everard Digby, did not enjoy it long because he was hanged for his part in the Gunpowder Plot. Crossing the Great Ouse river the trail winds through pleasant villages and woods until it crosses into Bedfordshire and reaches Olney. This handsome little town was the home of the melancholy poet William Cowper and the Rev. John Newton, slave trader turned evangelist who wrote the hymn *Amazing Grace*. They have a museum in Cowper's house. Passing through Threeshires Wood, where three shires actually meet, the route follows Forty Foot Lane, an old Roman road, to the remains of a Norman castle at Yielden, before crossing over a ridge of higher ground into Cambridgeshire. On the last section it goes through Calpher Wood, first recorded back in 1271, and finally encircles Graffham Water, an important place for rare bird species.

Olney Church from the Three Shires Way

TWO MOORS WAY

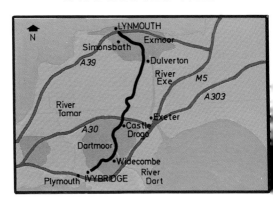

Length:	102 miles 163 kms
Status:	Regional route
From:	Ivybridge
To:	Lynmouth
Terrain:	Open moorland, some boggy, steep hills, wooded valleys
Maps:	OS Landranger 180, 191, 202
Access:	BR Plymouth and bus. A38 Exeter-Plymouth road BR Minehead and bus. A39 North Devon coast road
Route Guides:	*Two Moors Way* by H.Rowett (Devon Ramblers' Association)
Information:	Dartmoor National Park Authority, Bovey Tracey, Devon Exmoor National Park Authority, Dulverton, Somerset

This crosses the only two national parks in southern England and calls for some hillcraft and map reading skills on the moorland sections. In a few places a compass bearing will be the only thing to follow because sometimes, despite some thick green lines on the 2½" maps, there is little to see on the ground in the form of definite tracks. Wisely the authorities have not intruded waymarks where these would be inappropriate to the landscape. The start from Ivybridge immediately launches the walker into a steep climb up the valley of the River Erme on to Dartmoor which abounds with prehistoric huts, stone circles, megaliths, medieval clapper bridges, old tin workings, etc. Soon the trail finds the River Dart, queen of the many Devon rivers, and follows it up to several towering granite tors before cutting across to Widecombe-in-the-Moor famed for Uncle Tom Cobley. Passing over Hameldown the track comes to Grimspound, the extensive remains of a Bronze Age village (no fences, no entrance fees). For a while the Two Moors Way is coincidental with an ancient route called the Mariners Way whose origins are obscure. It then enters the valley of the River Teign where the outstanding landmark is Castle Drogo designed by Lutyens for a millionaire grocer. Leaving Dartmoor there is a day's march across the farmlands of mid Devon before climbing again to the heights of Exmoor whose boundaries run right down to the coast. Though there are some stiff climbs Lorna Doone's country is less wild and broken than that of Dartmoor.

Sharp Tor, near Castle Drogo

VIKING WAY

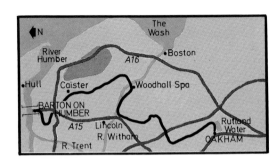

Length:	140 miles 225 kms
Status:	Regional route
From:	Humber Bridge
To:	Oakham
Terrain:	Flat or very gently rolling farmland and fen
Maps:	OS Landranger 112, 113,117, 121, 130, 141
Access:	BR Barton-on-Humber. A15 from south, A63 from north BR Oakham. A606 Melton Mowbray-Oakham road
Route Guides:	*The Viking Way* (Lincolnshire County Council) *Viking Way* by R.Stead (Cicerone Press)
Information:	Lincs County Council Recreational Services, Newlands, Lincoln

Nobody is pretending that Vikings actually followed this trail, but they pillaged the surrounding countryside and their memorials are mainly in the place names. Later invaders left more tangible monuments in churches, villages, and ancient trackways which will be enjoyed on this trek across one of England's biggest counties. It is also one of the flattest so the going is never hard . The northern terminal is at the end of the road bridge across the Humber Estuary and the river is followed to South Ferriby before heading south for the quiet villages of the Lincolnshire Wolds, via the market town of Caister which still has its Roman walls. As the trail approaches Woodhall Spa it is possible on a clear day to see Lincoln Cathedral, over 20 miles away, rising high on a limestone bluff from the surrounding fenlands. Into Lincoln and out of it the path follows the River Witham through the fens and across Lincoln Heath, once notorious for footpads and still an isolated place. The towpath of the Grand Union Canal eventually takes the route over the boundary of what used to be Rutland, England's smallest county now merged with Leicestershire. A lot of it was flooded to make Rutland Water, the huge artifical lake whose northern shore is followed to take the Viking Way into Oakham, the former county town which traditionally demands the forfeit of a horseshoe from every peer who passes through. Hundreds are on view in the 12th century Castle Hall.

Lincoln Cathedral, a landmark for miles   *(Photo: Jarrold Publishing)*

WAYFARER'S WALK

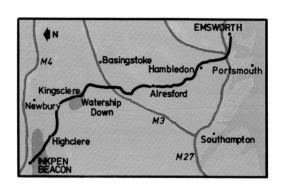

Length:	70 miles 112 kms
Status:	Regional route
From:	Inkpen Beacon
To:	Emsworth
Terrain:	Chalk downland, field paths and old tracks. Steep beginning
Maps:	OS Landranger 174, 185, 196, 197
Access:	BR Kintbury via Reading. M4 junction 13 BR Emsworth. On A27 south coast road
Route Guides:	*The Wayfarer's Walk* by Linda Herbst (Hampshire County Council)
Information:	Hampshire County Council Recreation Department, North Hill Close, Andover Rd, Winchester SO22 6AQ

Hampshire means coast to many people, but it is a big and varied county stretching north almost to the Thames. The Wayfarer's Walk runs diagonally across its expansive acres from the boundary with Berkshire to the sea. Inkpen Beacon, the starting point (or finish), is the highest chalk hill in England, 974 ft above sea level with sweeping views. It is crowned with a gibbet, scene of a gruesome local legend, and also an Iron Age fort. Descending from the heights the walk passes Highclere Castle, home of the Earls of Caernarvon, one of whom discovered Tutankhamun's tomb and is buried on nearby Beacon Hill. Pleasant walking over springy downland round Kingsclere crosses Watership Down, noted for its racehorse training gallops and setting for Richard Adams' novel of the same name. Part of an old Roman road called the Portway makes the next stretch, leading to the broad Georgian main street of Alresford. This is the half-way mark and a trip on the Watercress Line, a restored steam railway, makes a pleasant break here. The way south is along the valley of the River Itchen, a noted trout stream, and eventually along a series of ancient trackways till you reach the salt marshes and mudflats of Langstone Harbour. Following along its shores towards Hayling Island leads to another deep sea inlet, Chichester Harbour. Emsworth is an attractive little town at the head of one of its creeks. It is possible to make a big triangular circuit of Hampshire, going back along the Solent Way and the Test Way (q.v.).

Gibbet on Inkpen Hill

WEALDWAY

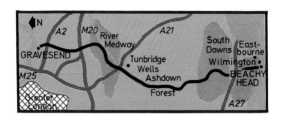

Length:	80 miles 128 kms
Status:	Regional route
From:	Gravesend
To:	Beachy Head
Terrain:	Undulating downs and woodland. Mostly firm and dry
Maps:	OS Landranger 177, 188, 198, 199
Access:	BR Gravesend. A2 out of London BR Eastbourne. Off A259
Route Guides:	*Wealdway Long Distance Footpath* (Ramblers' Association) *The Wealdway* by K.Reynolds (Cicerone Press) *A Guide to the Wealdway* by J.H.N.Mason (Constable)
Information:	Ramblers' Association, 1, Wandsworth Rd, London SW8 2XX

Weald simply means forest, which covered in ancient times much of the parts of Kent and Sussex explored by this trail. It is still very leafy country. The parts that are not are mainly chalk downland which makes a good contrast. The first two miles from Gravesend pier see the built up area left behind at Sole Street and the path then begins to climb up to the North Downs from where it looks down a strangely shaped valley called Bewley Alley. It descends the southern slopes through Wrotham Heath and Meredith Woods, the largest remaining expanse of woodland in Kent. At West Peckham it enters a Rowland Hilder landscape of hop fields and oast houses. By way of contrast it then follows the riverside path along the Medway to Tonbridge which has many old buildings and a castle. Staying with the river the trail reaches the Sussex border near the Forest Way Country Park. Just ahead the path enters Five Hundred Acre Wood, part of the Ashdown Forest, where you can find the very bridge on which Winnie the Pooh and Christopher Robin invented the game of Pooh Sticks. A.A. Milne lived close by. Leaving the forest the path winds through arable lands to begin the climb up the South Downs. From the far slopes, looking out over the twisting Cuckmere Valley, there are glimpses of the sea. A strange sight on the way is the Long Man of Wilmington, a primitive hillside chalk figure of unknown origin. Eastbourne is a seaside town retaining a faintly Edwardian air and soon after the trail ends on the high chalk cliffs of Beachy Head.

In the Kentish weald

WEAVERS' WAY

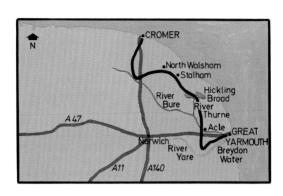

Length:	56 miles 90 kms
Status:	Regional route
From:	Great Yarmouth
To:	Cromer
Terrain:	Waterside paths, flat farmland and coast
Maps:	OS Landranger 133, 134
Access:	BR Great Yarmouth. A45 from Norwich BR Cromer. A140 from Norwich
Route Guides:	*Weavers' Way* leaflet (Norfolk County Council)
Information:	Director of Planning, County Hall, Norwich NR1 2DH

Though the starting and finishing point are both on the sea this is not a coastal walk. Instead the path meanders through the more interesting and attractive hinterland. Once it was an area where weaving flourished as a cottage industry, but it lost out to big mills elsewhere after the invention of the power loom, for which walkers can be thankful because what remains is a string of unspoilt villages. The Weavers' Way also passes through the heart of Britain's newest national park, Broadland, taking in scenes of Arthur Ransome's two Broads based adventures, *Coot Club* and *Big Six*. From Great Yarmouth the path heads along the embankment of Breydon Water, a great place for watching waders, wildfowl and migrant birds. Then it crosses Halvergate Marshes, an area so important to wildlife that landowners are paid to keep traditional methods of farming. Turning northwards the path follows the River Bure through Acle until it is joined by the River Thurne just below Potter Heigham, where the popular amusement is watching hire cruisers negotiating the very low and narrow 14th century bridge. Beyond is the Thurne windpump which has been draining the marshes since 1820 and is open to the public. Still following the river the trail reaches Hickling Broad, also an important water nature reserve. There are many fine flint churches and several notable stately homes before the trail comes to an end with the highest church tower in Norfolk at Cromer. This is one of the four trails to make up the Around Norfolk Walk (q.v.).

Thurne Mill by the Weavers' Way   *(Photo: Jarrold Publishing)*

WEST HIGHLAND WAY

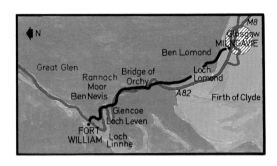

Length:	95 miles 153 kms
Status:	National trail
From:	Milngavie
To:	Fort William
Terrain:	Moderate hills to start followed by rough lochside paths, mountain slopes and exposed open moor
Maps:	OS Landranger 41, 50, 56, 57, 64
Access:	BR Milngavie via Glasgow. A809 from M8 junction 6 BR Fort William. A82 from Glasgow
Route Guides:	*West Highland Way* by R. Aitken (HMSO) *Guide to the West Highland Way* by T.Hunter (Constable)
Information:	Scottish Countryside Commission, Battleby, Redgorton, Perth PH1 3EW

Most long distance trails can be walked in either direction, but the West Highland Way demands to be walked only one way, from the south. Striding from the Lowlands to the heart of the Highlands, from the edge of industrial Glasgow to the foot of Britain's highest mountain seems the only fitting thing to do.

The scenery grows more superb with every step. The first day's walk is a gentle breaking-in through woods and low hills to the southern end of Loch Lomond. Then the route follows close to the eastern shore of Scotland's biggest loch for 20 miles, scrambling over the lower slopes of Ben Lomond. This is the territory of the outlaw Rob Roy whose cave is seen at Inversnaid. A real climb into the hills begins here, but the way makes use of old drove roads and military roads built after the '45, so the track is often smoother and easier to follow than you might expect on high moorland. There are nevertheless long stretches of exposed country beyond Bridge of Orchy and over Rannoch Moor with no habitation. The village shop at Tyndrum is the last for 19 miles. An 800 ft zig-zag climb over a pass called Devil's Staircase, ends in Glencoe, brooding still on its infamous massacre 300 years ago. After the glen the track stays on high ground, around 1,800 ft till it reaches the head of Loch Leven. There are only 15 miles to go now to Fort William and Ben Nevis is in sight. It is not on the way, but for those with the energy left the path to the 4,000 ft summit starts only a mile or two further on.

Glencoe on the West Highland Way   *(Photo: Ian Howard)*

WEST MENDIP WAY

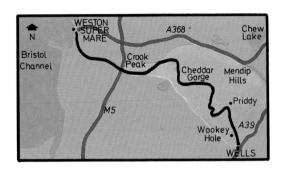

Length:	30 miles 48 kms
Status:	Regional route
From:	Wells
To:	Weston-super-Mare
Terrain:	Hill ridges and limestone gorges, steep and rough in places
Maps:	OS Landranger 182
Access:	BR Bath Spa and bus. A39 from Bath BR Weston-super-Mare. M5 junction 21
Route Guides:	*West Mendip Way* by A.M. Eddy (Weston-super-Mare Civic Society)
Information:	Tourist Information, The Gorge, Cheddar, Somerset BS27 2QE

The Mendip Hills have some punishing gradients, but once on top the climber is rewarded with splendid ridge walks and sweeping views. Between the hills dairy pastures and limestone villages make a complete contrast and there are some spectacularly deep rock gorges. This trail across the Mendips begins in Wells near the majestic west front of the cathedral. Soon it reaches Wookey Hole, a complex of huge caves which were once desirable residences for prehistoric man and are now a tourist attraction. It then enters the quieter Ebbor Gorge, a steep climb but a good place for spotting birds of prey. The village of Priddy at the other end has earth circles of unknown antiquity and the remains of Roman lead mining activity. After a woodland interval there are more steep climbs to reach Jacob's Ladder, high above the famous Cheddar Gorge which is a towering rocky defile, riddled with caves and a prime tourist attraction. Walkers are soon spared the crowds by climbing a wooded nature reserve to Black Rock. From here the way drops to Shipham and joins an old drove road leading on to Wavering Down, over several stretches of 'gruffy ground', a local term for land scarred by old lead mining. On a clear day the Welsh mountains and Exmoor can be seen from here. Flanking the summit of Crook Peak ahead the trail descends past a working wheelright's workshop and museum to cross a bridge over the M5. After some lesser gradients it reaches the Bristol Channel at Uphill, close to the sands of Weston-super-Mare.

Cheddar Gorge in the Mendips

WOLDS WAY

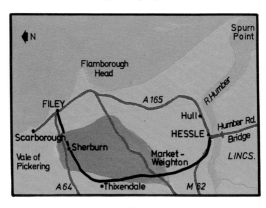

Length:	79 miles 127 kms
Status:	National trail
From:	Hessle Haven
To:	Filey
Terrain:	Gently rolling farmland, smooth hills and dry valleys
Maps:	OS Landranger 100, 101, 106, 107
Access:	BR Hessle. Off A64 road to Hull or Humber Bridge from south BR Filey. Turning off A64 from York
Route Guides:	*The Wolds Way* by R.Ratcliffe (HMSO) *The Wolds Way* by D. Rubinstein (Dalesman Publications)
Information:	Technical Services Dept., Humberside County Council, County Hall, Beverley HU17 9XA Yorkshire and Humberside Tourist Board, 312 Tadcaster Rd, York YO2 2HF

A part of rural Yorkshire (natives don't accept Humberside) that contains rewarding walking away from major tourist traps. The start is among the mud flats and fens of the Humber, from Hessle Haven close to the northern end of the Humber road bridge. The trail initially follows the river for a few miles before turning inland for North Ferriby, then through a belt of woodland as far as Welton where the long arm of the law at last caught up with Dick Turpin in 1739. After South Cave the flat estuary lands are left behind and the country rises gently to open wolds which pastured huge sheep flocks until a generation ago, but are now mostly arable. A diverging path to Market Weighton makes a convenient overnight stopping place. Part of an old Roman road provides the next part of the trail as far as the parklands of Londsborough Hall. Around Warrendale are expansive views from the heights as far as distant York Minster, then a string of pleasant villages marks the way to Thixendale at the halfway mark. The second half is through even more peaceful country, looking from the escarpment of the wolds over the Vale of Pickering to the moors beyond. The village marked on the map as Wharram Percy can't be relied on for refreshment. It was deserted after the Black Death around 1350. There is a last climb over Staxton Wold and Flixton Wold before the first glimpse of the North Sea. Most walkers are content to finish on the tide washed reef called Filey Brigg, but the end is a mile further at Newbiggin Cliff.

Kilnwich Percy Hall, Wolds Way   *(Photo: Humberside County Council)*

WORCESTERSHIRE WAY

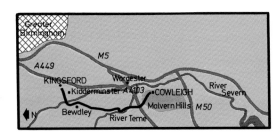

Length:	36 miles 58 kms
Status:	Regional route
From:	Kingsford
To:	Cowleigh
Terrain:	Gently rolling farmland, woods and stream paths
Maps:	OS Landranger 138, 150
Access:	BR Stourbridge and bus. Off A442 from Kidderminster BR Malvern Link. A4103 from Worcester
Route Guides:	*Worcestershire Way* leaflet (Hereford & Worcester County Council)
Information:	Countryside Officer, County Hall, Spetchley Rd, Worcester

Not long as county trails go, but enough for a varied
week-end. It marches south from the Kingsford
Country Park which covers 200 acres of heath and
conifer. An old English patchwork of small fields and
birch woods is then crossed to Shatterford where there
is a view of the distant Clee Hills. The way now
descends into the Severn Valley and after passing
through Eymore Woods reaches a series of reservoirs

at Trimpley where ospreys have been seen. Following the river downstream the trains of the Severn Valley Railway will be seen steaming through the woods on the other bank. This brings the route to Bewdley, a Georgian town with a river frontage and a brass rubbing centre. The way out of the town follows the Coffin Route, along which in times gone by the dead had to be carried for burial at Ribbesford. At Abberley a huge Victorian clock tower dominates the village. After Walsgrove Hill old orchards and steep pastures follow a limestone ridge to Ankerdine Hill before the trail drops into the Tene valley. On crossing the river to the far side there is Ravenshill Wood, a nature reserve. Hop fields and oast houses make this part look like a corner of Kent. The way now straggles up the Suckley Hills and down to Birchwood Common where Sir Edward Elgar composed the *Dream of Gerontius*. His beloved Malvern hills are in view and though the trail ends at their foot few will resist the temptation to do the last couple miles to the summit of Worcestershire Beacon.

Worcestershire Way ends at the foot of the Malvern Hills

WYE VALLEY WALK

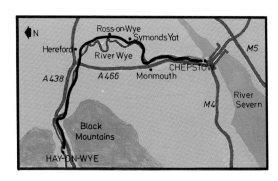

Length:	75 miles 120 kms
Status:	Regional route
From:	Chepstow
To:	Hay-on-Wye
Terrain:	Level riverside paths with steep rocky passages between
Maps:	OS Landranger 149, 161, 162
Access:	BR Chepstow. M4 junction 22 BR Hereford, then bus. Off A438 Hereford-Brecon road
Route Guides:	*Wye Valley Walk* pack (Wye Valley Countryside Service)
Information:	Wye Valley Countryside Service, Hadnock Rd, Mayhill, Monmouth, Gwent NP5 3NG

The Wye must surely rate as one of the loveliest rivers
of Britain, despoiled almost nowhere. Consequently
the Wye Valley Walk is wholly delightful. Chepstow
Castle, the starting point, is an imposing pile built to
stake a claim to the troubled borderlands within a year
of the Norman Conquest. From the town the route uses
paths laid out by an 18th century landowner to provide
ten different views of the river. Then it climbs 700 ft

above to the Eagles' Nest from where it is said that you can see seven counties. An old pack horse track takes it to Tintern Abbey whose ruins inspired Wordsworth to verse. Tintern railway station has also been preserved and the walk follows the track of the defunct Wye Valley Railway. Monmouth, slightly off the track, is a fine town well worth a diversion. Upstream the valley sides become steeper and more wooded as the walk approaches Symonds Yat. The views here are spectacular, especially if you climb Yat Rock, a dizzy height shared by peregrine falcons and birds eye orchids. The river is now on the edge of the Forest of Dean, but the path shortly crosses over it to Welsh Bicknor and Goodrich Castle, on its way to Ross-on-Wye and the cathedral city of Hereford. Scenery on this stretch reverts to wide, level meadows, but soon reaches low hills again, passing through the parishes of the diarist parson Francis Kilvert. There are then moorland tracks into Hay-on-Wye and a link with the Offa's Dyke Path (q.v.).

The Wye Valley from Yat Rock

TRAILS CLASSIFIED BY AREA

Scotland
Southern Upland Way (coast to coast)
Speyside Way (Grampian region)
West Highland Way

Wales
Coed Morgannwg Way (South Wales)
Glendower's Way (Mid Wales)
Offa's Dyke Path (north to south)
Pembrokeshire Coast Path (West Wales)
Wye Valley Walk (S.Wales and Herefordshire)

Northern England
Centenary Way (Mid Yorkshire)
Cleveland Way (North Yorkshire)
Coast to Coast Walk (Lake District & North Yorks)
Cumbria Way (Lake District)
Dales Way (Yorkshire Dales & Lake District)
East Riding Heritage Walk (East Yorkshire)
Lyke Wake Walk (North Yorkshire)
Pennine Way (Derbyshire, Yorkshire,
Northumberland)
Sheffield Way (South Yorkshire)
Wolds Way (East Yorkshire)

Midlands
Cotswold Way (Gloucestershire)
Greensand Ridge Walk (Bedfordshire)
Heart of England Way (Staffs, Warwicks, Glos.)
Nene Way (Northamptonshire)
Oxfordshire Way
Robin Hood Way (Nottinghamshire)
Sandstone Trail (Cheshire)
Severn Way (Gloucestershire)
Shropshire Way
Staffordshire Way
Three Shires Way (Bucks, Beds, Cambs)
Worcestershire Way

Eastern England

Angles Way (Norfolk)
Around Norfolk Walk
Essex Way
Hereward Way (Cambridgeshire)
Peddars Way (Norfolk)
Viking Way (Lincolnshire)
Weavers' Way (Norfolk)

Southern England

Greensand Way (Surrey and Kent)
Imber Range Perimeter Path (Wiltshire)
Isle of Wight Coast Path
Kennet & Avon Canal Path (Berks, Wilts, Avon)
King Alfred's Way (Hants, Berks, Oxon)
London Countryway (all the Home Counties)
North Downs Way (Surrey and Kent)
Ridgeway (Bucks, Berks and Wilts)
Saxon Shore Way (Kent)
Solent Way (Hampshire)
South Downs Way (Hampshire and Sussex)
Stour Valley Walk (Kent)
Swan's Way (Buckinghamshire)
Test Way & Clarendon Way (Hampshire)
Thames Path (London, Surrey, Berks, Oxon, Glos.)
Wayfarer's Walk (Hampshire)
Wealdway (Surrey and Kent)

South West England

Cornwall Coast Path
Dorset Coast Path
Leland Trail (Somerset)
Saints Way (Cornwall)
Somerset & North Devon Coast Path
South Devon Coast Path
South West Peninsula Coast Path (Somerset,
Cornwall, Devon, Dorset)
Two Moors Way (Devon)
West Mendip Way (Somerset and Avon)

TRAILS CLASSIFIED BY LENGTH

	miles	kilometres
South West Peninsula Coast Path	560	896
Cornwall Coast Path	268	431
Pennine Way	250	402
Around Norfolk Walk	220	352
Southern Upland Way	212	341
London Countryway	205	330
Thames Path	195	314
Coast to Coast Walk	190	304
Pembrokeshire Coast Path	180	290
Offa's Dyke Path	168	270
Saxon Shore Way	143	230
North Downs Way	141	227
Viking Way	140	225
Glendower's Way	125	200
Shropshire Way	125	200
Cleveland Way	108	172
King Alfred's Way	108	172
Two Moors Way	102	163
Cotswold Way	100	161
South Downs Way	99	158
West Highland Way	95	153
Peddars Way	93	150
South Devon Coast Path	93	150
Staffordshire Way	92	148
Robin Hood Way	88	141
Kenneth & Avon Canal Path	86	138
Ridgeway	85	137
Somerset & N.Devon Coast Path	82	132
Centenary Way	82	132
Dales Way	81	130
Essex Way	81	130
East Riding Heritage Walk	80	128
Heart of England Way	80	128
Wealdway	80	128
Wolds Way	79	127
Angles Way	77	123

	miles	kilometres
Wye Valley Walk	75	120
Dorset Coast Path	72	116
Nene Way	71	113
Cumbria Way	70	112
Wayfarer's Walk	70	112
Isle of Wight Coast Path	67	108
Oxfordshire Way	65	105
Swan's Way	65	105
Weavers' Way	56	90
Greensand Way	55	88
Solent Way	55	88
Severn Way	50	80
Test Way & Clarendon Way	46	73
Speyside Way	45	72
Sheffield Way	45	72
Hereward Way	43	68
Lyke Wake Walk	40	64
Greensand Ridge Walk	40	64
Stour Valley Walk	38	60
Saints Way	37	59
Three Shires Way	37	59
Worcestershire ay	36	58
Sandstone Trail	30	48
Imber Range Perimeter Path	30	48
West Mendip Way	30	48
Leland Trail	28	44
Coed Morgannwg Way	27	43

Many trails link with others to make a longer walk, or in some cases to provide a shorter circuit or a return route. Useful main links are mentioned in the trail descriptions, but space does not permit them all to be listed.

A FEW TRAIL WALKING TIPS

How Far In A Day?

Needless to say the answer depends on individual experience, temperament and the type of terrain. A 20 mile day is quite feasible for fit adults in all but very hilly country, but a daily target of around 15 miles makes for a more relaxed holiday with time to sit and admire the view and explore places of interest. In planning itineraries allow for extra miles at the beginning and end of the day for getting to and from your accommodation point or transport. Distances given in guide books refer only to the mileage on the actual route.

Safety

Most of the walks reviewed here are without dangers, but precautions should always be taken on those crossing mountain and high moorland country.

* Take a map and compass and know how to use them.
* Inform relatives of your itinerary and phone an 'all-well' message when you reach your evening base.
* Have adequate spare warm clothing and iron rations like glucose tablets or Kendal mint cake.
* Carry a torch and a whistle.

What To Take

If you haven't walked long distances before make sure you do so in footwear that has been broken in. Walking boots are essential in hill country both for ankle protection and the grip the soles have on slopes but on lowland trails stout shoes are adequate for those who prefer them. Thick wool stockings are the most comfortable.

Walking all day means that you'll need to carry fully waterproof protective clothing, not just showerproofs. Headgear for extremes of weather is desirable even if you don't normally wear hats. For body warmth several thin layers are better than one big thick jumper.

Dehydration causes discomfort more quickly than hunger so take plenty to drink. Apples are very refreshing and provide enough energy to keep you going for miles.

Finding The Way

The word 'waymark' is mentioned frequently in this book. Don't expect a huge sign. Waymarks are intended to be discreet little symbols, not an eyesore in the countryside. Usually they appear only where there is a change of direction or tracks diverge. Some trails have their own distinctive waymarks but elsewhere the recognised standard is a litle yellow arrow, or a blue one if the path is also a bridleway. They supplement the 'public footpath' fingerposts which are mostly where paths leave a road. So keep alert eyes for waymarks. If you go astray simply consult the map, cast around a little and you'll soon pick up the trail again. If there is a danger in the long distance trail idea it is that we may all end up being molly-coddled by officialdom. Walkers should be prepared to use a bit of initiative. Nobody wants the countryside turning into a municipal park. There is an old rambler's saying: "He who has never been lost has never been far".

Rights of Way

Trails mostly follow 'rights of way' which are very ancient institutions by which people have gone about their lawful business in the countryside since time immemorial. Anyone has a legal right to pass peacefully along them, but on foot only. It is illegal for farmer or landowner to obstruct path or user.

Bridleways are also rights of way but may be used by horse riders and cyclists as well as pedestrians.

Britain has 140,000 miles of right-of-way footpaths. They are constantly under threat from vested interests and the best way to preserve this priceless national heritage is to use them.

USEFUL ADDRESSES FOR GENERAL INFORMATION

Ramblers' Association, 1 Wandsworth Rd, London SW8 2XX

Long Distance Walkers Association, 7 Ford Drive, Yarnfield, Stone, Staffordshire, ST15 0RP

Youth Hostels Association, 8 St Stephens Hill, St Albans, Herts AL1 2DY

Camping Club of Great Britain, Greenfields House, Westwood Way, Coventry CV4 8JH

Countryside Commission, John Dower House, Crescent Place, Cheltenham, Glos. GL50 3RA

Countryside Commission for Scotland, Battleby, Redgorton, Perth, PH1 3EW

Council for the Protection of Rural England, 25 Buckingham Palace Rd, London SW1X 8PQ

British Tourist Authority, 64 St James St, London SW1.

English Tourist Board, Thames Tower, Black's Rd, London W6 9EL

Scottish Tourist Board, 23 Ravelston Terrace, Edinburgh EH4 3EU

Wales Tourist Board, 2 Fitzalan Rd, Cardiff CF1 3NQ

British Travel Centre, 4 Regent St, London SW1Y 4PQ

National Trust, 42 Queen Anne's Gate, London SW1H 9AS

National Trust for Scotland, 5 Charlotte Square, Edinburgh EH2 4DU